GOD'S PATTERN
for
PARENTAL NURTURING

PASTOR GBOLAHAN BRIGHT

Unless otherwise indicated, all Scripture quotations are taken from the King James Version of the Bible.

First publication
GOD'S PATTERN FOR PARENTAL NURTURING
© 2017 Pastor Gbolahan Bright

Printed in United Kingdom

ISBN-978-1-5136-2501-0

All rights reserved.
No part of this publication may be re-produced, stored in a retrieval system or transmitted, in any form or by any means without the prior permission in writing of the author or as expressly permitted by law, or under terms agreed with the appropriate reprographics rights organisation.

Enquiries concerning reproduction outside the scope of the above should be sent to the author. You must not circulate this book in any other binding or cover, and you must impose this same condition on any acquirer.

Cerint Media
www.cerintmedia.com
+44(0)7502373695

DEDICATION

This book is dedicated to the ANCIENT OF DAYS for HIS grace upon my life, family and ministry.

CONTENTS

Acknowledgement vii

Foreword ix

Preface xvii

Introduction 23

Chapter One
The Home (The Foundation Of Nature And Nurture) 27

Chapter Two
Creating The Right Atmosphere For Child Bearing And Child Rearing 37

Chapter Three
Understanding Parental Responsibilities 45

Chapter Four
Character Building (The Journey To Self Identity) 61

Chapter Five
The Place Of Prayer And Spirituality 97

Chapter Six
The Relevance Of Vision 109

Chapter Seven
The Right Counsel (Avoiding The Seat Of The Ungodly) 123

Chapter Eight
Leaving A Good Legacy 135

Conclusion 141

ACKNOWLEDGMENT

First and foremost, I give glory to the Almighty God for making this dream a reality; indeed, it is a dream come true. 'God's Pattern for Parental Nurturing' is one of the most challenging assignments I have undertaken in recent times. A lot was invested into it in terms of effort and time. Contributions from brethren both far and near are also noteworthy and commendable.

Consequently, I would like to take this opportunity to express my profound gratitude to the vision helpers who played fantastic roles in making this book a mission accomplished. These wonderful people include:

Our General Overseer Pastor EA Adeboye and Pastor Mrs Folu Adeboye, for their spiritual covering and teaching.

Every "Aaron and Hur", particularly members of the RCCG, The Masters Sanctuary, Dagenham Essex for their moral and spiritual support.

My darling wife Councillor Afolasade Bright and our lovely children for their outstanding support.

My biological parents Mr and Mrs E. O. Bright for the nurturing I receive from you from time to time.

A special thanks to Barrister Wemimo Ogunde (SAN), Rita Eluwade, Tele Adewusi and sister Funke Adaramola for their hard work in typing, proof reading and design of this book.

This acknowledgment will be incomplete without mentioning the inspiration, invaluable advice and prayers I receive from time to time from my mentors Pastors: Francis Oladimeji, Seyi Oladosu , Anu Ojo, Bola Lawal , Olalekan Akinleye and Yemi Adesanya. I appreciate you all. May the presence of God never elude any of you, your light will never diminish or become darkness in Jesus Name, Amen.

And of cause to my publisher, Pastor Lauretta Amata Olowu, for the typesetting, design and publishing of this book. May the Lord bless you richly for making this book a reality in Jesus Name.

My prayer is that God will settle you all in Jesus' Name ! Your labour of love upon my ministry shall not be in vain in Jesus Name; SHALOM.

FOREWORD

In a time when all we know as Christians and parents is challenged and questioned, a book such as 'God's Pattern for Parental Nurturing, by Pastor Bright Gbolahan becomes much-needed medicine and a breath of fresh air for parents who believe that nurturing of their child to overcome their journey of life is important.

A book in this category must be welcomed now when Christian values are debated and watered down by most governments and powers in our global communities.

What Pastor Bright, aims to achieve in writing this book is to remind parents and leaders, that the child needs continuous nurturing even when they become young adults. The upbringing continues to be their support network.

This book also reminds parents, that a child encounters difficulties he must overcome at each stage of his life by the support he gets from their parents.

Pastor Bright is a notable man of God, who preaches the word of God with simplicity and love.

He is a husband and a father who himself has applied most of the principles in this book, as they have been revealed to him by God (Dan 2: 21-23).

Pastor Bright's words of encouragement and mentoring encapsulate the work of intercession that was done by Daniel in the scripture mentioned above. Not only has Pastor Gbolahan Bright been given an opportunity to nurture young persons who are wiser than their age; he shares these secrets with as many parents that come his way.

Like Daniel, Pastor Bright continues to stand firmly on his belief that God makes the unknown to be known to an individual. He mentors parents and leaders in the community on what they need to do to enhance the academic and spiritual performance of their children and young people. A lot of the work he has done with parents is reflected in this book.

Many parents who have come in contact with this humble teacher have learnt some basic truth about the abilities of their children even when those were not obvious.

Having had the opportunity to read this book, I can

FOREWORD

already foresee how this book would make a positive impact on parents and their children across the globe.

Pastor Bright is a man who believes there is no limit to the greatness in a child if they are nurtured to overcome challenges in their journey of life.

I have known Pastor Bright for some years; he carries a grace that does not undermine any individual; he sees beyond what is physically present in a child.

He says "if parents are ready to work, the child would be a true testimony for all to see". Pastor Bright is a perfect candidate to write a book like this, having shown us that a child can pass GCSEs at age 10 and graduate from the university at age 17.

A book like this is a must read and must be applied by all parents and leaders.
I say 'applied' because Pastor Bright is passionate about applications of formulae and principles. He truly loves people, and he takes their concerns to heart and assists whenever he can. So once again, I encourage all parents to reach out and get a copy of this book and apply the principles in the book and by the grace of God you will see positive changes in your home and children.

Rita Eluwade

What is so impressive about Pastor Gbolahan Bright MBE is that he combines within himself, three persons. First, he is a Christian leader, who is noted for his deep spiritual insight and biblical ethics. Secondly, he is an exemplary father and thirdly a trained and informed mathematician, with extensive knowledge.

He teaches, mentors, trains and writes not as an armchair theorist, but as someone God has allowed to have practical experience in all three areas, minister, father, and lecturer. He takes readers into his confidence, shares his experience from a biblical perspective, and expects them to make up their minds on each issue based on biblical evidence.

His well-grounded faith informs all of his thinking. In response to the increasing demand on his time from outside RCCG (Redeemed Christian Church: The Master's Sanctuary), Pastor Bright resigned from full-time lecturing, to enable him to work on projects that involve reaching out to help, love and support those in need, in particular, the young people.

As a full-time minister, Pastor Bright is well aware of how satan has kept young people in bondage. He is sensitive to their silent cry for help and the yearning to be free from drugs, alcohol, sexual immorality,

FOREWORD

lack of parental love and guidance and ignorance of gospel truth. As a solution to some of the challenging problems the secular world throws at us, Pastor has written this influential book as a way to tackle persistent and growing problems. In this book, he seeks to explain the message of Christianity and to relate his biblical worldview to the complexities of the modern world.

Pastor Bright is a father with all the duties, responsibilities and vulnerability that is associated with fatherhood. That is why he can empathise and enter into other people's experience of pain. He has the unpleasant task of telling parents that their son/daughter needs love. Then he weeps with those who weep. He does not underestimate the seriousness of the ongoing attack on Christian families and the body of Christ.

Pastor Gbolahan Bright's love and integrity shine through this book from the very first page to the last. He does not conceal the truth about disturbing facts, nor does he evade serious questions. He offers solutions to complex contemporary problems not based on man's ideas or opinions but solely from the direct word of God. He publicly espouses the need to bring up children in a Godly way, so that in later life they will not depart from the truth.

Pastor Bright is hugely influential, albeit in a very modest way. He is widely respected and admired and is motivated by the godly ambition to restore hope, love and faith to this generation to lead a global revival in basic Christianity. The task of parents is to protect and nurture their children in line with God's intentions.

This book is a 'must read!'

Dr. Elizabeth Negus FcoIIT FRSA
Chairman of Board of Trustees,
(RCCG The Master's Sanctuary)
Member of NLC Commonwealth Committee
Advocate for Chartered College of Teaching

FOREWORD

There has not been a more critical and urgent time, in recent decades, when the need for such a book as **"God's Pattern for Parental Nurturing,"** is more pertinent and, arguably, imperative and most relevant book to parents and guardians.

This book is a blessing to parents who grew up in a generation knowing nothing about biblical parenting, those who are trying to improve in their parenting, those who are in the verge of giving up and those who want to go the biblical foundations of parenting.

In our world today, more than ever, our children and most especially, the family unit is under heavy spiritual attack. As Christians, we need spiritual and practical ways to help us nurture our children as God so designed from the beginning.

In recognition of the challenges faced by parents and guardians in raising up their children in godly way, Pastor Gbolahan Bright, has succeeded through this book in providing hope and help for them.

With each chapter, Pastor Bight succeeded in communicating to us, the word of truth from the introduction of the topic, useful instructions, guidelines, with prescribed prayer points for parents and their children.

If you implement these biblical principles and practices as Pastor Bright has designed in this book, you are sure to raise godly children that will bring glory to God.

Pastor Lanre Peters
Zonal Coordinator, RCCGNA NY -10

FOREWORD

There has not been a more critical and urgent time, in recent decades, when the need for such a book as **"God's Pattern for Parental Nurturing,"** is more pertinent and, arguably, imperative and most relevant book to parents and guardians.

This book is a blessing to parents who grew up in a generation knowing nothing about biblical parenting, those who are trying to improve in their parenting, those who are in the verge of giving up and those who want to go the biblical foundations of parenting.

In our world today, more than ever, our children and most especially, the family unit is under heavy spiritual attack. As Christians, we need spiritual and practical ways to help us nurture our children as God so designed from the beginning.

In recognition of the challenges faced by parents and guardians in raising up their children in godly way, Pastor Gbolahan Bright, has succeeded through this book in providing hope and help for them.

With each chapter, Pastor Bight succeeded in communicating to us, the word of truth from the introduction of the topic, useful instructions, guidelines, with prescribed prayer points for parents and their children.

If you implement these biblical principles and practices as Pastor Bright has designed in this book, you are sure to raise godly children that will bring glory to God.

Pastor Lanre Peters
Zonal Coordinator, RCCGNA NY -10

PREFACE

Why This Book?

Writing this book taught me a great lesson – never give up on your dream; it's just a matter of time. In fact, I had almost given up because of the lack of motivation along the way. What stirred me up again or reignited the drive was my recent experience as a foster carer with the London Borough of Havering. It was quite a revealing experience. After all, as they say, experience is the best teacher. One thing that stood out from these diverse experiences is the fact that as an individual you cannot operate beyond the amount of light (knowledge) available to you at a time. If you want to be distinguished in any area of life, never undermine the importance of knowledge.

Indeed, understanding is the key; understanding is what makes you outstanding.
Collectively, from my experience as a foster carer, it is obvious that some parents have missed it right from

the very beginning. They have no clue about what parenting is and sadly their children are at the receiving end. These children bear the brunt of the ignorance and mistakes of their parents. What is more disturbing and disheartening is the fact that children from supposedly Christian homes are also caught up in this messy situation. Also, apart from misplaced priorities, some parents/guardians are not conscious of the prevailing circumstances of this end-time which the Bible describes as evil. Unlike the sons of Issachar who understood their time and acted accordingly 1 Chronicles 12:3, the reverse is the case with some parents no wonder the story remain the same that is, the struggle continues, that will not be your testimony in Jesus Name.

However, for this to become a reality as an individual you must step up your work with God, dig deep into **His Word** and put your trust on Him and not on your position, title or riches.

In a nutshell, this book is a clarion call to us as parents and guardians to put our house in order for the sake of posterity. For some of us, as a starting point, we must put off the mask of insincerity and hypocrisy, admit where we have missed it and genuinely make amends. The earlier we take this bold step, the better for our children and Nation at large. Enough of passing the

PREFACE

bulk because of it's attendant consequences.

I will like to use the story of a minister of the Gospel to drive home this point. He kindly gave me the permission to use it as a lesson for Christians who are in the business of chasing shadows to the detriment of reality.

He is a dynamic Pastor whose church was formerly based in East London. He is a family friend, and one can consider him a success if material gains and the size of the church were the parameters to define who has made it in the ministry. At the time of this story, he was in full-time ministry with his lovely wife. To them, ministry was 24/7, as they were so involved in church activities to the detriment of their children. Simply put, they didn't have time for a stable connection with their children. Consequently, these vulnerable children were at the mercy of social media influence and ungodly relationships. Before they knew it, their son was excluded from secondary school for a period of time.

Instead of facing reality, my Pastor friend decided to play the race game. He felt that his son was a victim of racial discrimination and didn't admit the fact that there was a lack of parental support and involvement with his son. To worsen the situation, the boy denied committing the offence he was accused of when repeatedly asked by his parents at home. However, on the appointment day with the Head teacher and Class teacher, this boy admitted the fact that he was the culprit. It was a huge embarrassment to this man of God because he didn't expect it at all. This reinforced the fact that a child left on his own will bring shame to his parents. It was a shameful experience, and the tragedy of this story was the remark the head teacher made afterwards. Simply put, he told my friend without mincing words that the only people he sympathises with are the members of his church. He wondered what type of message a man who cannot manage his home, could have for the body of Christ.

Who says unbelievers do not know the scripture. The truth, as they say, is bitter but must be said. This open rebuke hit this man of God and this time he made the right decision. He admitted he was guilty of negligence of duty and asked for forgiveness of his sin. This incident was the turning point in the life of this wonderful family. There are lessons to learn from stories like this as some children have ended up in prison due to a continuous negligence and nonchalant attitude of their parents.

For example, in the Uk a recent review on Black, Asian and Minority Ethnic (BAME) published by David Lammy MP, on 8 September 2017 shows that the proportion of BAME young offenders in custody has

PREFACE

risen from 25% to 41% between 2006 and 2016, and also the proportion of young people offending for the first time rose from 11% in 2006 to 19% a decade later. It was also revealed that black children are more than twice as likely to grow up in a lone parent family, and black and mixed ethnic boys are more likely than white boys to be permanently excluded from school. *https://www.gov.uk/government/news/lammy-publishes-historic-review*. My prayer for you is to be blessed through the revelation shared in this book.

In Ephesians 6:4, the words, "bring up," are from the Greek word 'ektrefw' which means, "to nurture, nourish, provide for with care that nourishes, feeds, or trains." In other words, we are to provide the kind of care that will promote healthy growth and development. Of course, the context is dealing with spiritual and moral development that flows out of a right relationship with God, walking under God's control, but it is the fruit of the loving care of godly parents.*https://bible.org/seriespage/6-principle-nurture-training-your-child*

Nurturing is an exciting but demanding process, and in this book, I have attempted to break the process down into simple chapters for better understanding. However, what this book is saying may not make sense to you, if you are not born again. The starting point of excelling as a parent is to be a child and a friend of God.

Although this book is targeted at Christian parents, it is important to note that parents with moral decorum and upbringing tend to discover and grow personal resilience. As they do this, they grow a deeper understanding of the impact they have on their children. When resilience is built up in the children, they can weather the toughest storms in life and make the most of the opportunities that life presents.

Please note also that this book will be referring to parenting from the perspective of married couples bringing up their children together. It, however, does not exclude Christian widows or widowers, single parents or divorced, guardians, etc. who are bringing up their children alone. We learn from the Bible that Timothy was mainly influenced by his grandmother Lois and His mother, Eunice. We also see that in spite of her plight as an eventual single parent, God still came to Hagar's rescue.

May your effort over your children be sweet in Jesus Name Amen.

Happy reading.

Pastor Gbolahan Bright

GOD'S PATTERN FOR PARENTAL NURTURING

Introduction

The master plan of God for mankind is to reflect His beauty and glory. At the beginning of creation, God created all things with a command—*"Let there be..."* And there was. But when it came to the creation of man He said *"Let us MAKE man in our image after our likeness"* (Genesis 1:26) Therefore, of all the entities created by God, man was the only one he moulded after His image. This is because He wants man to have Him as a standard and grow up to be a glory 'carrier'. God made us as the clay, poured us out as milk, and curdled us like cheese. He clothed us with skin and flesh and fenced us with bones and sinews" (Job 10:11)

Man is indeed a masterpiece of creation!

Therefore in all facet of human existence, God wants to use humankind to show forth His glory particularly in parenting.

Frederick Douglas said, *"It is easier to build strong children than to repair broken men."* Parents need to understand that nurturing and guidance are important in transforming children into proper adolescents. It becomes a mirage once they become adults! Hence the Bible counsels that you should 'train up (or build-up) a child in the way he should go, and when he is old, he will not depart from it.' – (Proverbs 22:6). The challenge is that if we are not equipped and ready to see them built up to our desired image (which should be consistent with God's plan for the children), the world and satan (will do the job and build them up to the undesirable image.

To be successful in parenting, we need to be on the Lord's side. We need to give our lives completely to Him, to be called by His name. This is the beginning of Godly parenting.

If we surrender our lives to Christ, the Son of the living God, we will receive direct instructions from Him and have our children become 'a peculiar people'.

INTRODUCTION

The apple of Gods eyes! They will become an enviable point of reference, record - breakers in their generation and a compelling voice in their respective communities.

When we study the ancient Greeks and Romans, we discover that "when their family life was strong and vibrant, so too were their societies and civilizations". *http://www.annunciationwoburn.com/assets/files/Articles%20by%20Father%20Peter/cnc.pdf*

The Jews also understand kingdom dynamics. They do not see themselves less than how God sees them. They are the sons and daughters of the Lion of the tribe of Judah! They are constantly following God's instructions as commanded in Deuteronomy 6:7, nurturing their children with the Word of God.

Therefore if we desire our children to excel in life, if our aspiration for them is to be a force to be reckoned with, and if we desire them to be greater than us, so that they will arise as great icons in the society, then they need to be well nurtured to overcome in the journey of life. This journey begins with you as a parent.

James E. Faust said, *"To be a good father and mother requires that the parents defer many of their own needs and desires in favour of the needs of their children. As a consequence of this sacrifice, conscientious parents develop a nobility of character and learn to put into practice the selfless truths taught by the Saviour Himself."*

This, in a nutshell, is the main objective of this book.

CHAPTER ONE

The Home
(The Foundation of Nature and Nurture)

THE HOME is the foundation of nature and nurture. It is the place where the child inherits his genes and cultivates his habits. Nature has to do with the genetic components of a person, which is received during conception, while nurture is the cultivated component acquired during training. The home is the environment where these components interact to form character, and character can either bring victory or defeat in the journey of life.

The home is the product of the marriage. It takes a good marriage to produce a good home, and it takes a bad marriage to produce a bad home. The nature of the home will determine how the child will be nurtured to enable him to overcome in the journey of life. This is also true of the Animal Kingdom. For example, the home of a tamed rabbit is called a hutch, while that of a wild rabbit is known as a burrow, even though they are both rabbits. The difference is in the taming- the nurture and nature. In the same vein, a house can be as huge as a castle and as impressive as a skyscraper, and still not qualify as a home. Whereas another house can be as tiny as a matchbox, and be located in a slum, but still qualify as a home. The difference between them is not in their location or size, but the atmosphere of warmth, love and togetherness that exists in the place.

The warmth and togetherness existing in the home is a function of the relationship subsisting between the husband and the wife, who have a deep understanding of the reason why they have been joined in marriage. Without this understanding, divorce, separation and strife will be the order of the day.

Loving relationships and happy children don't just happen; they need nurturing, openness and information. From pregnancy through birth and the bringing up of children, knowing the facts can dispel anxiety of bringing up children.

God has ordained marriage for a specific purpose. Until that purpose is understood, the home will be unable to nurture the child to overcome in the journey of life. A lot of divorcees are always quick to say, "Oh, we married for the wrong reasons!" Could there be any other valid reason for marriage, but the God-given reason?

Genesis 2:18 says *"It is not good for a man to be alone; I will make him a help meet for him..."* And verse 24 further says *"Therefore shall a man leave his father and his mother, and shall cleave unto his wife: and they shall be one flesh"* The word "Therefore" means "For this reason". Therefore, in Matthew 19:5 Jesus reiterated this, and said: *"For this cause..."* i.e. for this reason *"... Shall a man leave father and mother and shall cleave to his wife: and the twain shall be one flesh."*

From the above passages, we can rightly deduce that the ONLY reason given by God for marriage is to make "AN HELP MEET" FOR THE MAN, TO RID HIM OF HIS 'ALONENESS.' This is the truth, and it is very fundamental to the "why" of marriage. This truth is the foundational framework and platform upon which the home is built. The Bible says you shall know the truth and the truth shall make you free. The truth is foundational. It has a voice which cannot be suppressed. From experience, it has been discovered that anything not anchored on the truth cannot stand the test of time. It will appear to disappear.

This is the bane of most broken homes today-faulty foundations occasioned by marriage for the wrong reasons!

According to the research by Care for the Family through their project 'Home for Good', over 50 children are relocated daily into care in the UK. They are removed from confused, hurtful, offensive circumstances the children erroneously call 'home'. Many children need a new home; some others need a temporary home until they can go back to their respective families.

Beloved parents, your children are as strong as their foundation. It is the foundation that determines the nature and nurture of a child because the home is the bedrock of parenting. Man has been empowered to produce "after his kind." In 2 Kings 21:19-20, we are told of a king called Amon. The Bible says *"...And he did that which was evil in the sight of the Lord as his father Manasseh did."* (italics mine). As parents, you give what you have and not what you lack. Your children reflect your nature, and the nurture you give them.

Parents need to know that one important feature of virile families is to have family tradition. I am talking about customs and rituals the families repeatedly do.

Activities like eating dinner together; attending events together every Saturday; reading the Bible together before going to bed and many others. These are the things that help to bind families together in one accord.

The raising of children is nothing but a physical and emotional rollercoaster! That is why parents should be given all the essentials they can get to support them through the challenges of being parents and to keep their own relationship robust.

Therefore, to make your home a strong foundation for parenting, your marriage must be in line with God's standard. In Genesis 26:34-35, Esau married outside God's standard, and the marriage was a *"grief of mind unto Isaac and to Rebecca."* May your children's marriage not bring you grief in Jesus Name. Marriage outside God's standard brings nothing but pain and regret. God's standard for your marriage is the real and sure foundation of a solid home.

The standard of God is Jesus Christ the solid Rock. In Matthew 7: 24-29, Jesus told the story of the builders. One built upon the sand and the other upon the rock. Both buildings experienced the storms of life. But what made one fall and the other stand, was their foundations: "...And the rain *descended, and the floods came, and the winds blew and beat upon that house, and it fell not: for it was founded upon a rock..."*

Upon what is your home founded? The vicissitudes of life are common to every man, but the ability to overcome and forge ahead will depend on the foundation upon which he stands, and that foundation is Jesus Christ... *"For other foundation, can no man lay than that is laid, which is Jesus Christ"* (I Corinthians 3:11).

It is little wonder then that many pastors have recommended Edward Mote's hymn on foundation, as one of the key hymns for wedding programmes. The impact of that song is still as profound today as it was in the generation of the song writer.

Before we consider how to build on the foundation, it would be helpful to sing that song and meditate deeply on it to further illuminate our understanding of foundation. The song is titled "The Solid Rock."

THE SOLID ROCK

1. *My hope is built on nothing less
   Than Jesus' blood and righteousness;
   I dare not trust the sweetest frame
   But wholly lean on Jesus name.*

THE HOME (THE FOUNDATION OF NATURE AND NURTURE)

Chorus
On Christ, the solid rock I stand
All other ground is sinking sand
All other ground is sinking sand

2. *When darkness seems to veil His face*
   I rest on His unchanging grace.
   In every high and stormy gale
   My anchor holds within the veil

3. *His oath His covenant His Blood*
   Support me in the whelming flood;
   When all around my soul gives way
   He then is all my hope and stay

4. *When He shall come with trumpet sound*
   Oh, may I then in Him be found
   Dressed in His righteousness alone
   Faultless to stand before the throne.

However, it is not enough to lay a foundation; we must make efforts to build on it. Foundation without consolidation will not bring the expected reward. Many parents have laid their homes on Christ the solid rock, but are using wrong materials to build the home and by extension the lives of their children. To be faultless to stand before the throne of judgement is to be careful how we build the home. 1 Corinthians 3:10 & 13 says *"...But let every man take heed how he buildeth thereupon. ...and the fire shall try every man's work of what sort it is."*

Beloved parents, how are you building your homes? Are you building the lives of your children with straw, woods, and stubble? Or are you building them up with gold, silver and precious stones? The Bible says, *"Every man's work shall be made manifest....And if any man's work abides which he hath built thereupon, he shall receive a reward."*
Therefore, to have bountiful rewards, you must be careful how you bring forth your children and how you nurture them.

An article titled **The Christian Family: Nurturing Children in The Lord by Arie den Hartog** a Missionary of the Protestant Reformed churches vividly captures what nurturing a child involves he says:
"The nurturing of our children involves much more than merely objectively teaching them the truth of the Word of God. We must train them actually to live the Christian life. We must show them what it means to love the Lord and keep His commandments. We must admonish them, exhort them, rebuke them, encourage them to live as Christians;

we must compel them, motivate them, urge them on. We must foster in them a proper spiritual attitude concerning themselves. We must encourage them when they are discouraged and help them through periods of depression and sorrow.

We must teach them to live as mature, responsible Christians on their own, build them up in such a way that they can make moral judgments and discernments on their own. We must warn them of the serious consequences of sin and teach them to fear the holy and righteous God in the way of obedience before Him." https://standardbearer.rfpa.org/index.php?q=nod e/48422

I pray for you that as a parent God will give you great reward as you nurture your child according to His Word.

GOD'S PATTERN FOR PARENTAL NURTURING

PRAYER POINTS

1. Blood of Jesus purge the foundation of my home and correct every fault programmed to destroy it in Jesus Name

2. Anywhere my home has been deformed, disarranged and disorganised, oh Lord arise, repair and correct it. Let the powers that have vowed to turn my home upside down receive perpetual reproach in Jesus Name.

3. Let the fire of the Holy Ghost cut off the pattern of suffering and hardship programmed into my home from my family line.

4. May the roof over my children's head never be removed in Jesus Name.

5. The blood line of the blood of Jesus round my home will never be removed in Jesus Name.

6. My home will not be a death trap to my family and me in Jesus Name.

7. Oh Lord make my home a safe haven for all my children in Jesus name. Oh Lord, remould my home to carry your divine agenda. Make it a citadel of your glory and power in Jesus Name.

CHAPTER TWO

Creating The Right Atmosphere For Child Bearing And Child Rearing

"CHILD Bearing" is to incubate and bring forth children. "Child rearing" is to raise, tend, train and nurture the child. To bring forth a child requires adequate preparation. To "rear" a child requires sufficient knowledge, skill, time and efforts.

Many times in the Bible, it is recorded when a special child is about to be born, God gives the parents specific instructions on how to prepare for the arrival of the child. As parents, you can also key into this pattern to bring forth unique children. The Bible says, *"Train up a child in the way he should go, and when he is old he will not depart from it"* (Proverbs 22:6).

The Bible says, "train" not "teach" not "lecture." This means you are to raise the child, tend, tame and nurture the child in the way acceptable to God. Training is a process. You cannot do this without creating an enabling environment.

Raw materials needed to build on the solid foundation include being a manager who sets good examples. Parents should seriously consider what the children will become. Parents cannot afford to get it wrong.

It is not enough to just bear children. What is the value of having children who cannot confront life's challenges? Therefore, as parents, you must create the right atmosphere for the children you are about to bring to the world. We are in a corrupt generation; a world full of gender crisis, fraud, alcoholism, cultism, wickedness and all manner of depravity. For your children not to be caught in these negative influences, it is imperative to create the right atmosphere in the home for their upbringing, so that when they grow up, they can easily discern what "should be" from what is already practised in the world.

Having children and raising them is a massive and enduring commitment. It is a commitment to being the father and mother to the children while still alive.

CREATING THE RIGHT ATMOSPHERE FOR CHILD BEARING AND CHILD REARING

You can NOT switch off! You never stop being a parent at any time. This is worth thinking of before taking the irreversible dive of having children.

HOW DO YOU CREATE THE RIGHT ATMOSPHERE?

1. Nurture your hearts with the Word of God. This is the starting point. The General Overseer of the Redeemed Christian Church of God (RCCG), Pastor E.A. Adeboye, has often said that whether your children will have a smooth ride in destiny or not will depend largely on your relationship with God. To nurture your children effectively, you must first nurture your own heart with the Word of God. There are no delinquent children but delinquent parents! The Bible says, *"you, therefore, who teach another, do you teach yourself? You who preach that a man should not steal do you steal?"* (Romans 2:21).

Many parents today are the direct opposite of what they want their children to be. I counsel you to know God intimately before you teach your children about Him. You cannot give what you don't have. As parents, we must set godly examples for our children because we are meant to be their positive role model, as action they say speaks louder than words. Every parent must know that their sons and daughters discover what to do by observing what they do.

2. Daily commit your home into the hands of God. Marriage is a journey, with twists and turns. Commit that journey into the hands of Him who knows the end from the beginning. He is faithful to keep that which is committed to Him until that day.... (the appointed day of glory). Commit the agenda of your home into His hands, your lives, business, career, unborn children, EVERYTHING! Be a PRAYING COUPLE. Spirituality gives direction. The Bible says: *"Trust in the Lord with all thine heart and lean not unto thine own understanding. In all thy ways acknowledge Him, and He shall direct thy path"* (Proverbs 3:5 & 6). I advise you to commit your everyday lives into the hands of God and trust Him with your home. He will bring all your desires to pass.

3. Have love and respect for each other as a couple. Be sweet to your spouse. You cannot hate your spouse and expect love in return. You cannot disrespect your spouse and expect honour in return. Love and respect are mutual and contagious. Show your spouse uncommon love (1 Corinthians 13:7), and you will receive uncommon love in return. Love and respect are about deposits and withdrawals. You can't withdraw what you have not deposited. Whatever deposits you put into your union as a couple will transform into an investment for your children tomorrow, and they too will value their spouses. Charity begins at home!

CREATING THE RIGHT ATMOSPHERE FOR CHILD BEARING AND CHILD REARING

4. Decide together the number of children you can reasonably bear and rear. It is true the Bible says your quiver will be full of arrows. But what is the value of arrows that cannot defend you at the gate against the enemies? (Psalm 127:4&5). Here the Bible is talking about quality and functional arrows. It is the quality of life you give your children, and not the number you produce, that will determine their functionality in life. Gideon had seventy children, but a bastard child arose and killed sixty-nine of them, almost returning him to where he started from. Jochebed had three; All three had colourful destinies-Aaron (the High Priest) Miriam (a prophetess), and Moses (the deliverer). There are some families where ten sons are not equivalent to one child, and there are others, where one child is like having more than ten sons. Samuel seemed like an only child to his parents, even though Elkanah his father had more than five children. (1 Samuel 1:4 & 2:21)

5. Appreciate God for the seed and gender in your womb. The sex or number of your children has nothing to do with their success or failure in life. What determines their success or failure is the quality of life you give them. A daughter can be to her parents what ten sons cannot be e.g. Deborah. Solomon had multiple wives, but only one son succeeded him and eventually ruined his legacy - Rehoboam.

6. Speak greatness to the unborn child every day. The prayer that revealed to Rebecca, that she was carrying two nations in her womb, was certainly not a casual prayer. It was born from an unbroken relationship with Jehovah. Start moulding the destiny of your children from the womb. They can hear your voice. The baby leapt for joy in Elizabeth's womb when he heard the salutation of Mary. (Luke 1:44). Tell God what you want them to be right from the womb. The Bible says they are for signs and wonders. Be intentional about speaking scriptures over your unborn child, as *"we know that the Word of God accomplishes the purpose for which it was sent"* (Isaiah 55:11-12).

Here are two examples of scriptures you can use to pray for your unborn child:

> *"I have no greater joy than this, to hear of my children walking in the truth."*   3 John 4

> *"All thy children shall be taught of the Lord, and great shall be the peace of Thy children."*   Isaiah 54:13

7. Forsake not the gathering of the brethren. Husbands must encourage their pregnant wives to attend prayer meetings organised for pregnant women. Some churches have a set time for this. There are specific corporate prayers for pregnant mothers which can only be received in such gatherings.

CREATING THE RIGHT ATMOSPHERE FOR CHILD BEARING AND CHILD REARING

8. Make physical and medical preparations for the unborn child. Set money aside and attend ante-natal clinic with your wife. Buy clothing, and prepare the cradle cheerfully for the baby's arrival. It is the lack of preparation and planning that makes a young man panic when his wife is in the labour ward. Proverbs 24:27 says *"Prepare thy work without, and make it fit for thyself in the field and afterwards build thy house."* Planning is key to creating the right atmosphere for bearing children.

The arrival of a child into the home makes a huge demand on both parents, individually and collectively. The child becomes the central focus in the house as all activities will naturally revolve around him/her. To handle this stage effectively, parents need to understand their roles in child care.

PRAYER POINTS

1. Lord let the strife of tongues and satanic discussions targeted to stifle and scatter my home come to an end in Jesus Name.

2. Oh Lord restore the broken relationship and heal the broken trust in my home in Jesus Name.

3. I decree that anointing for fruitfulness multiplication and dominion shall envelop my home in Jesus Name.

4. I cut off every flow of hereditary problems into the lives of my children in Jesus name. No child born into this family shall inherit the evil of our family lines in Jesus Name.

5. I speak wellness and wholeness into the lives of every child born into this family in Jesus name. No child passing through my womb/produced from my loins shall have any deformity or disability in Jesus name. I speak perfection into your body organs and systems. Your position at birth shall be head downwards. Your arrival shall be without complications. I shall not run from pillar to post because of you. Your entrance into this home shall usher in peace prosperity and all round favours in Jesus Name.

6. Oh Lord, let divine resources to take care of my children and home overshadow me in Jesus Name.

7. May the presence of the Living God overshadow my home and make my home a fertile ground for fruitfulness and divine harvests.

CHAPTER THREE

Understanding Parental Responsibilities

If you want to produce godly seeds for a better tomorrow and you want to have rest and bountiful rewards in your old age, it is important as parents to understand your roles and responsibilities towards your children.

There are four kinds of parenting:
1. Biological -Abraham/Isaac
2. Natural -Naomi/Ruth
3. Foster -Mordecai/Esther
4. Spiritual -Paul/Timothy

In whatever category, you find yourself as a parent; God wants you to give it your best. Therefore, whether you are a Mordecai, an Apostle Paul, a Naomi, or an Abraham, you are a parent. You are a father and a mother to your ward, and God is asking you to rise to your responsibilities. You will give a personal account of your stewardship to Him.

Beloved parents, parenting is a joint responsibility. The desire of God is for every parent to raise God-fearing children. "...That he might seek a Godly seed." (Malachi 2:15) When He comes to your home seeking, will he find such godly seeds?

For God to find godly seeds in a home, parents must nurture their children together and not separately. Though the role of each spouse in the home is different, they often overlap. Most fathers think their only responsibility is to provide financial support for the family. This is just one facet of God's demands from you as a father. A proper understanding of your responsibilities will determine the kind of children that will emerge from your home. Jarius understood this. So, he sought help from Jesus, for his daughter's healing, while his wife stayed back home to take care of her (Luke 8:41-56). It was a joint effort. Jesse sent provisions to his sons on the battle field, through David, while his wife (Nahash- 2 Samuel 17:25) probably stayed home. (1 Samuel 17:17). It was the same for Jacob who asked Joseph to check on his brothers. (Genesis 37:14)

The responsibilities of the father go beyond money. You must be there for your children. Now let's examine the father's specific duties

THE DUTIES OF THE HUSBAND/FATHER

The Husband/Father is created for headship. (Genesis 3:16; 1 Corinthians 11:3; Ephesians 5:23). He is the head and General Overseer of the family. As such a lot is expected of him as the captain of the ship.

a. He is the spiritual Head and Leader of the home
b. He Provides for the Home
c. He is a Mentor and Teacher
d. He is a Disciplinarian
e. He protects and shields the family
f. He is a friend and companion to the family

THE DUTIES OF THE WIFE/MOTHER

Proverbs 14:1 says, "Every wise woman builds her home. But a foolish woman plucks it down with her own hands."

The woman's role is that of a home builder
a. She is a helper and support to her husband
b. She is a home maker

c. She is a companion
d. She is a teacher and trainer
e. She is a role model

Having an in-depth understanding of these roles makes parenting not only easy but interesting and desirable. The demands on each parent changes with the age of the child. But to play these roles effectively, the parents need one thing which is to be totally committed and devoted.

TOTAL COMMITMENT AND DEVOTION

Most parents do not have time at all for their children. They abdicate their responsibilities to house helps, drivers, nannies and grandmas, who in turn use their standards to bring up the children. However, to lay a proper foundation for nurturing the child, you must be committed and devoted to your children. People give attention to only what is important to them. Therefore, if your children are important to you, you won't need any sermon to give them attention. Parents spend quality time with your children by investing your time in the things that concerns them; this will help to build a strong bond and durable relationship.
Children are the heritage from God. They are God's responsibilities entrusted into your care. Therefore,

you will one day give an account of them to God. May you be faultless to stand in judgement before God in Jesus Name Amen.

WHAT DO COMMITMENT AND DEVOTION ENTAIL?

1. Commitment means making your children your priority. In the order of importance, your home comes first after God. Our God is a God of order; there is no chaos in creation. Some parents put their career, friends, social outings and public image before their homes.

As parents, your children are your priority no matter the challenge. Some parents never do the school run. They always depend on help from neighbours. This is wrong, and it would eventually breed contempt both for you and for that child! It's a matter of time. Some lock out their children when they are going out, and leave them to play with other children in the neighbourhood. The bottom line is this: If you can't take your children with you on a social outing then don't go! The ceremony would go on without you, and the gathering will be completed without your presence.

This is a fact of life.

If you are determined to struggle and labour to take your children to school with the scarce resources available to you, God will give you a car! Jacob was a man who placed a high premium on his family, and God enlarged his coast. In appreciation of God's mercies and prosperity, this was what he said: "With my staff, I passed over this Jordan; and now I am become two bands..." (Genesis 32:10). He left home with just a walking stick, but returned with two armies! So, shall the Lord enlarge your coast when you make your children your priority in Jesus name amen.

2. Commitment means being directly involved in the affairs of your children. Your children are your direct responsibility and personal programme. You take full responsibilities for them. You must not abdicate your responsibility to anyone else.

A good mother cannot be too busy to cook for her children and feed her babies. The only thing some mothers do, if at all, is to breastfeed. It is 'Happiness,' the nanny, who changes the diapers, sing lullabies to make the children sleep, dress them up for school, etc. No wonder some children are more comfortable in the company of their nannies than their own mothers! Commitment to your children connotes personal involvement in the affairs of the children.

3. Commitment means to be dedicated and loyal to your children. Be faithful to your children. Be reliable. Make them trust you. Let your words be your bond, such that they could take it to the bank, and it would be honoured! Some parents make promises they neither keep nor intend to keep. You are their model. If they can't trust you, who should they trust? Sometimes it may not be convenient to perform your words, but that's the enterprise of godly parenting. Integrity is doing what you should, or ought to do, even though it is not convenient.

4. Commitment means to invest in your children and support them. The Bible says: "A good man leaveth an inheritance to his children's children..." (Proverbs 13:22). Investment is a generational blessing. If you are not committed, you cannot invest, and if you don't invest in your own direct children, how can you leave an inheritance to your children's children? Today we hear of KFC, UNILEVER, and even back home in Nigeria PUNCH NEWSPAPERS, GUARDIAN NEWSPAPERS.

These are all investments laid down for generations yet unborn by their late founders. You must invest in your children. Spend time, energy, and resources on them. Nothing (within your reasonable capacity) should be too much to spend on your children.

Empower them for tomorrow. Some foolish men train their brothers, so their brothers can, in turn, help them train their children in future. This has never worked and will never work! When your brother grows up, he will naturally concentrate on his own nuclear family, not yours. So please be properly guided.

5.) Commitment means protecting and preparing your children for destiny. A classic example of this is Abraham. He gave ALL that he had to Isaac and gave gifts to the sons of his concubines, Hagar and Keturah. This would have been enough, to prepare them for destiny, but he took a step further, by sending all of them far away from Isaac, his son while he was still living. (Genesis 25:5-6).

Why did Abraham do this? He did this to protect Isaac, his son from adverse claimants. He did this to shield him from evil step-brothers that could want to encroach on his inheritance in the future. He prepared him for destiny. Abraham was a committed father! There is no nephew or niece you keep in your house that will not compete with your children, no matter how much you give to them. Therefore, it is important that you protect your children from oppression and unfair treatment.

Children are the heritage of God. They are God's treasures entrusted into your care, and you will one day give an account of them to God. Therefore, in order not to give a woeful account to God, it is important for you as parents to do all you can to nurture your children to overcome in the journey of life. Sometimes it becomes very tough and very challenging, especially for working mothers. However, you must understand how to balance your work demands and parenting, effectively.

Whatever category of parenting one belongs to, being a parent is hard work, but it is massively rewarding. Tips that can help make it worthwhile and make everyone in the family unit feel secure and loved include:

a. Recognise that each child is unique in abilities and personality.

b. Love each child as he or she is. Every child is different from the other child.

c. The self-esteem of the child should not be toyed with. Protect the child's self-esteem by speaking positive and emphasising how good and important the child is. Give room for discipline and encourage boundaries.

These make the child secure and to know how far the child can go in building a godly life. It teaches the child to have respect for other people.

d. Importantly, listen to your child. This is a crucial aspect where many parents are missing it. Some parents due to the way they were brought up, erroneously believe that children must only be seen and not to be heard. This however is the begining of communication breakdown between parents and children.

BALANCE YOUR CAREER AND PARENTING.

In life, everyone earns a living by selling something. You either sell goods, or you sell services. Your career is what you do to earn a living. To have a success story in life and parenting, it is important to earn a living. The glory of a man is in the work of his hands. However, your earnings alone cannot take care of the child.

What is the value of having much money without good children? That is why you need to balance your career with parenting so that you can have rest in old age. I pray for you that in the evening of your life, you will not be wrestling when you are supposed to be resting in Jesus name. Amen

HOW DO YOU BALANCE CAREER AND PARENTING?

1. Seek for divine direction. Proverbs 16: 9 says: "A man's heart deviseth his way: but the Lord directeth his steps." It is the daily steps that take a man through the way. Rather than devise your own ways, commit your steps to God. He is the one that gives the power to make wealth. If you commit your job and career to God, He will give you a valuable job that will make you a valuable parent.

2. Learn Time Management. Time, they say is the currency of life. The Bible says, "Redeeming the time, for the days are evil" (Ephesians 5:16). Some fathers don't leave work until their children lay down their heads to sleep. If you don't manage and apportion time to everything, time will manage you and disorganise you! "The key is to focus on a plan, get organised, and find the right balance between profession and parenthood." http://www.parents.com/parenting/work/life-balance/moms-balance-work-family/.

Ecclesiastics 3:1 says: "To everything, there is a season and a time for every matter or purpose under heaven." As parents, you must be like the men of Issachar, who had an "understanding of the times to know what Israel ought to do..." (1 Chronicles 12:32).

Therefore as career parents, you must be judicious with your time, if you are to balance career with parenting. Commit to meeting deadlines promptly, take initiatives with little or no supervision and always be on target with your job, so you can leave early to join your children at home.

3. Prioritise your children and make them your central focus. If you make your children your central focus, not all jobs will be appealing to you. This particularly goes for mothers. Any job that would distance you from your home and your children is valueless. A woman was transferred from Lagos to another state in Nigeria and left her husband and little children in the care of her cousin. The cousin who began to play the role of mother to her children invariably began to play the role of wife to her husband. She got pregnant and brought total confusion into the family.

Women be wise! "Money answereth all things" but does not give all things. It answers your need for a bed but cannot give you sleep. It answers your need for food but cannot give you appetite. It answers your need for a house, but cannot give you a home. Therefore, put your home in view when you are considering a job.

4. Maintain an unbreakable communication with your children while you are at work. Call and speak to each of your children, whether at home or in school, (where practicable). This must be done without affecting your effectiveness and productivity at work. Don't engage in the habit of being on the phone while at work. Perhaps, your break time which you are entitled to should be the appropriate time of calling.

It is not enough to speak to one child and assume all is well. Speak to each one of them. Randomly take a break from work and check on them without prior notice, whether they are at home or the day care/school. This would put them in check at home and thwart any unsavoury behaviour by the care givers/teachers at the day care centre/school.

5. Avoid useless socialising. Attend social functions when you really and truly need to be there. Some parents have their dairies filled with all manner of social and religious engagements at the expense of their children. In fact, it is after they have confirmed their attendance on the invite that they start worrying about where to keep their children, or who to stay with the children at home while they are away. Beloved parents, that party you have put above your children would go on, with or without you! God forbid anything happens to you on your way to the venue, the organisers and celebrants will refrain from acting on it, until the party is over! Please be wise and make your home your priority. A lot of children have been put into untold hardship because of this mindless decision.

6. Look for a suitable child care provider or child care centre. If you must get a nanny, do, but find them out by excellent references and track records, especially the day care centres. In fact, the care centres are most preferable. It gives room for collective attention and corporate control rather than leaving your child at the mercy of a single hand. Ask God to help you discern so you can make a good choice.

7. Plan and get organised. You get things done faster and properly if you plan. Pack your bags overnight and the children's school items. Have a mental note of what to do each day before the break of dawn. This keeps you on your feet and even makes you more resourceful and organised at work.

8. Create time for vacations and family outings. Taking time out to rest, rejuvenates you and increases family bonding. A lot of parents especially Africans, do not believe in vacations.

Sometimes they work for three years at a stretch without annual leave. This makes them burn out fast. But taking time out to go on vacation is a therapy on its own. It helps you balance your work and creates room for bonding with the family. The psalmist said, "You my soul come back to your resting place!" (Psalm 116:7)

9. Manage your stress and health. Take good care of yourself, so you don't break down. Find time to do medical check-ups to be sure you are fit and healthy. If you can afford an annual health screening, do. It's all about stress management, so you don't burn out unnecessarily. You are only a parent when you are alive!

In conclusion, the foundation of marriage will determine the nature of the home and end the atmosphere in the home will determine the nurture of the child. Nature and nurture work in tandem. It is the nature of the home that gives the capacity to nurture a child. Your child will be as strong as the foundation you give him. What makes a child miss home is not so much as the physical structures of the home, but the atmosphere that exists in that home, be it a room, a flat, a duplex, or a castle. The atmosphere or relationship existing between the father and the mother in the home is the bedrock of the child's nurture.

PRAYER POINTS

1. Oh Lord, my Father, arise and repair my faulty foundation and the foundations of my children (Psalm 11:3).

2. Any problem that I inherited from my parents which have been transferred to my children at conception, blood of Jesus purge them out, in the Name of Jesus.

3. Any satanic proverb and by-word, of "like mother like daughter, or like father like son, troubling the lives of my children be blotted out by the blood of JESUS (Ezekiel 16:44)

4. The rage of the enemies against the stars of my children shall not prosper in Jesus Name. (Matthew 2:2&3)

5. Power to train and nurture my children in the way of the Lord over shadow me in Jesus Name.

6. Oh Lord, my Father, as I begin to nurture my children, show me the road map to their colourful destiny in Jesus Name.

7. The anointing of Samuel for accurate reception of the Word of God, fall upon the lives of my children in Jesus Name. Amen (1 Samuel 3:10)

CHAPTER FOUR

Character Building
(The Journey To Self-Identity)

Character is the real you. It is what distinguishes you from another person. It is what the Bible describes as "the hidden man of the heart." Character is who you are when no one is watching. It is how you treat people who cannot fight back.. Many people who have dual or multiple personalities lack character. Character is the manifestation of your nature and nurture put together.

This means it is a combination of your inborn nature and acquired habits. It is formed by your daily actions which then become your habits and invariably becomes your character. Character development is not an event but a process. Therefore, every God-fearing parent is expected to build a strong Godly character into the lives of their children by determination and tireless commitment.

Character building begins from home (cradle) which is the foundation. The Bible says, "if the foundation be destroyed what can the righteous do?" (Psalm 11:3). This is why chapter 1-3 dealt extensively with the foundation of the home. Nothing fruitful can ever come out of a faulty or cursed foundation. Your foundation is the beginning of everything: how you met and married your spouse, how the children were conceived and born, how they were raised and trained, etc. All these are components of their foundation.

However, in this chapter, we shall be looking at building character in a child.

To build character in a child is to give him his self-identity. This is because character defines who he really is; it is his content- his core being. It structures the child's life and defines his success or failure in the journey of life. His identity is his trademark, and it will affect his destiny. Your identity is the picture you evoke in the mind of other people about yourself. When we think of Jacob in the Bible, the picture that comes to mind is the picture of a "supplanter." But when we think of "Israel" what comes to mind is the picture of "Strength, Faith, and Honour." Self- Identity is a function of character.

WHAT IS SELF-IDENTITY?

Life is a battle for destiny and the ability to make people know who you are will give victory in this battle. Self-Identity is the ability to know who you are and what you stand for. Many people do not really know who they are. That is why a lot of people today are suffering from identity crisis. They are always striving to be who they are not, or who others want them to be, and in the process, they get lost in the crowd and end up becoming a "Mr Nobody." Alice in Wonderland was once asked who she was; She said, "I don't know anymore...!" This is because she had transformed into different personalities within a space of time, which left her confused about who she truly was.

It is important for parents to understand their children's search for identity. It is a major challenge especially for a teenage child to find out exactly who he is, what he can do and what he is good at. Children are curious to know the group they fit into.

The personal identity of many people is shaped by the early experiences they have as children. Simple things like the words we speak into our children's lives can affect their self-identity.

The road to a child's self-identity begins with you as a parent. It is your ability to make your children become what God wants them to be, and not what you want them to be. You cannot accomplish this without divine help. "God created humans to have unique characteristics, and purpose. However, he designed us also to have a commonality of contentment with our lives through His will. We discover our true identity the more closely we are drawn to Him." *http://www.biblestudytools.com/topical-verses/bible-verses-about-our-identity-in-christ/*

Until God intervened, the identity of Jacob was in crisis. True self- identity comes from divine encounter. To help your child discover who he is, it is important to first get your priorities right as a parent.

GET YOUR PRIORITIES RIGHT.

A helper must be strong enough to help himself before he can stretch out a helping hand to another person. This is why when you board a flight you are advised during the safety announcements to always put on your oxygen mask first before attempting to help anybody else with theirs in an emergency.

To help your child discover his identity in Christ, you must:

1. Be a child of God yourself. You cannot teach them what you don't know. You must first nurture your own heart before helping the child nurture his heart. And this can only be done if you give your life to Christ. Godly parenting can only be achieved when you partner with God through His son Jesus Christ. And you cannot partner with Him in any task if you are still a sinner and living in your old Adamic nature. Amos 3:3 says, "Can two walk together except they be agreed?"

Raising Godly children requires godly wisdom and God is ready to assist you if you partner with Him by nurturing your heart to do His will always. How do you nurture your heart?

a. Be born again.
b. Wash your heart with the Word of God daily.
c. Delight yourself in God and commit yourself to a holy and righteous lifestyle.
d. Pray and fast regularly for your children.
e. Open your heart in total obedience to the leading of the Holy Spirit always.

2. Introduce God to your children very early in life. Build a God-consciousness in your children from the cradle. Let them know the sound of prayers even as babies. Let them tell the difference between the Bible and a story book.

However, if you have not nurtured your own hearts, you will lack the capacity to build a God-consciousness in your children or even familiarise them with the family altar. It is therefore important to first get your own priorities right so you can nurture your children to overcome in the journey of life. Make the church very attractive to them in such a way that whenever they are absent from church service, they become very uncomfortable, like fish out of water!

3. Involve your children in church activities and deposit the Word of God into them. Children have very impressionable minds. They rarely doubt you. Whatever you tell them they believe, even if you tell them you will buy them an airplane! Whatever they learn from the cradle, sticks to their hearts for a long time because their brains are like the computer!

That is why the Bible says that we should train up a child the way he should go, and when he grows up, he will not depart from it. Teach them the Word of God and let them memorise verses and chapters of Scriptures. You can start with very simple ones like, "thou shall not steal." and then go ahead to tell them the consequences of disobeying God's commandment.

4. Prayerfully lead your children to Christ and show them the way out of sin. It is not enough that they go with you to church and learn memory verses, or even get involved in church activities. They must have a divine encounter because salvation is personal. Let them say the sinner's prayers by confession, repentance, and forsaking their sins to follow Christ. By this, they will always be remorseful anytime they sin or disobey you or any constituted authority.

Most parents often take the above steps for granted. The mere fact that you take your children to church every Sunday does not mean they are born again. Going to church every day will not guarantee a Godly life-style unless you consciously involve them in the things of God and show them the way out of sin. To be successful at this, you must lead by example. You are their first teacher. Therefore, you cannot lead the way unless you know the way. You must get your priorities right!

With these priorities properly put in place, your children will begin to carve out their own personal identities that will empower them through life's journey. Self-identity is the first milestone that will help them chart the right course to their destination in life, despite the twists and turns they would encounter on the way.

Self-identity is a landmark that creates boundaries. It creates restraints and gives direction. When a man has sufficiently identified who he is, people will be careful what to throw at him! Self-Identity is the starting point to being unique. God has created each child unique and uncommon. No two children are the same including identical twins and Siamese twins. Each child is unique in his own right, just as the finger prints are unique to each person.

It is the uniqueness of each child that will deter-mine the building blocks required to make him conform to God's image. The fact that man was created in the image of God does not guarantee that he will continue in God's image in the journey of life. It requires a strong decision and focused determination. Therefore, as your children are growing, it is important to identify the building blocks unique to each child, so that your child can carry the image of God.

IDENTIFY THE BUILDING BLOCKS PECULIAR TO EACH CHILD.

Your child is unique, and so is his journey in life. Each child from your womb has a specific pathway ear-marked for him by destiny. 1 Peter 2:9 says, we are "...a peculiar people."

To nurture your child to overcome in the journey of life you must distinguish the traits or the dominant temperament peculiar to that child to enable you to use the right building blocks to mould him/her.

All children are different. We have the easy going and flexible or the active and strong-willed. We have the quiet and cautious. To recognise each child's temperament helps you to understand their behaviour and their perspective of life. This enables parent to work with and not against their children. Let it be clear to you, if you have more than a child, you have different personalities to contend with. Therefore, what works for one may not work for the other.

There are two basic building blocks available to you as parents.

1. The spiritual building blocks (General)
2. The physical building blocks. (Specific)

THE GENERAL SPIRITUAL BUILDING BLOCKS

1. WISDOM (The fear of God) – The fear of God is the beginning of wisdom and it is only fools that despise wisdom. (Proverbs 1:7). Teach your child to fear God. It is the fear of what God can do to a sinner that helps a child live a Godly lifestyle.

The bible says, "...And if the righteous scarcely be saved, where shall the ungodly, and the sinners appear?" (1 Peter 4:18). It is indeed "A fearful thing to fall into the hands of the living God (Hebrews 10:31). To build the fear of God into the heart of your children very early in life is the wisdom that will help them create the necessary boundaries in the journey of life, both at home and abroad.

2. VALIDATION-This is a process of parental approval, support and affirmation. Some parents treat their children anyhow, because of one challenge or the other; some because the child came as a girl, instead of a boy, others because of financial difficulties, disabilities, etc. Children are gifts from God. (Psalm 127: 3).
They are the fruits of your body. Your child needs the continuous assurance of your love and support. Your love and affection for him must continually be expressed, physically, emotionally, and spiritually. Love your child and let him know that you love him. When you validate a child, he glows and becomes more resourceful. Build up your child's confidence and let him know how important he is to you. Understand his peculiarities and relate with him based on your understanding.

Build confidence and self-esteem in him by the constant affirmation of your paternal and maternal protection.

Don't join others to condemn him or ridicule him in public. Draw him close and help him drive away his fears and doubts. Let him know he is a product of the King of kings and the Lord of Lords. Teach him to value his roots and the family name. If he values it, he will uphold the family values. The reason why a lot of children develop inferiority complex and low self-esteem all through life is because they have not been validated from the home.

Children who enjoy the support and the assurances of their parents stand tall and become great achievers in life. Gideon enjoyed his father's support. When the men of the city said to Joash his father, "...bring out your son that he may die..." because he had destroyed the altar of Baal in his father's house, Joash did not join the men to condemn his own son. Rather he said to them: "...will you fight for Baal...? If he is a god let him fight for himself because someone has destroyed his altar!" This is parental validation. Where other parents would have chickened out, Joash stood firmly behind Gideon, his son.

However, this does not mean parents should not know where to draw the line. They should be honest and courageous enough to stop their children from going into error especially in choices detrimental to them e.g. marital choices, career choices, etc. Therefore, foundation cannot be over emphasized.

3. INVESTMENT- Your time with your children is your greatest investment. Time is the currency of life. Spend quality time with your children because "...a child left to himself bringeth his mother to shame." (Proverbs 29:15). Spend money and resources on them. Help them discover who they are and what they are created to be. Help them discover the signs and wonders they have been created for (Isaiah 8:18). Prepare them for their purpose in life and help them steady their focus on their vision. Nothing should be too much to pay for them to actualize their destiny.

4. DISCIPLINE. Proverbs 29:15 says, "The rod and reproof give wisdom: but a child left to himself bringeth his mother to shame" You can only bend the stick when it is still fresh. Children are great manipulators! Don't let them manipulate you by making you overlook their faults all the time. The Bible says, "Foolishness is bound in the heart of a child, but the rod of correction shall drive it far from him." (Proverbs 22:15). However, the rod of correction is not a hundred-inched pole! Yes, it is true that "When thou beatest him with the rod he will not die..." (Proverbs 23:13). The rod here is not just the physical rod.

Some parents have caused permanent damage to their children for lack of wisdom. The rod is not a leather whip, lashed on their backs with the force of hatred and uncontrollable anger! Know the correct rod to use. Understand the language of your child, and handle him with empathy, as you had once been a child yourself. Colossians 3:21 says, "Fathers provoke not our children to anger lest they be discouraged." Therefore, as you use the rod, be sure you also have the staff in your other hand to comfort them and not to crush their spirits.

It is very vital for parents to come into agreement on the disciplinary issues. Do not give room for the children to play one of you against the other. Parents should always present a united front and support one another when discussing the issue of discipline.

5. COMMITMENT- Accept them as your top priority. Plan for them, provide for them and plan your life and activities around them until they become independent. For instance, you don't plan your life around a gainfully employed adult. Make your children your personal programme as they grow. God will hold you responsible for them.

6. PRAYER- Prayer is the most powerful force in the universe. Prayer helps when all else fails. Take each one of them to God in prayer. When praying for them, treat them as separate and collective entities before God. Many parents have the habit of asking God to please, "take care of my children." This is wrong. Call them by their names before God. They all have different destinies. That is why God says He knows our names (Isaiah 43:1). When Jacob prayed for his children, he called each one of them by name and blessed them (Genesis 49:1-28). When Moses prayed for Israel, he prayed individually for them before a collective prayer (Exodus 33:6-29). The Bible says Job prayed for his children and *"offered burnt offerings according to the number of them all."*

Your prayer is activated more when you go on your knees to pray specific prayers for every one of your children. Christian history would be incomplete without Susannah Wesley. She was a known prayer warrior. She interceded every day on her knees, one hour for each child. Today she is celebrated as the mother of the Methodist Brothers! - John and Charles Wesley, founders of the Methodist Church. Make an effort to set out specific time to pray for your children daily. May your children make positive impact in history in Jesus Name Amen.

THE SPECIAL PHYSICAL BUILDING BLOCKS

Recognising that each child is unique and different (even when they are twins), will help you identify the special building blocks required to build the child. Each special building block comes with its own demands. They are properly so called, because they are not only peculiar to the child but are physically exerting, with time in view. The special physical building blocks are employed subject to the age, gender, and temperament of the child. This means that the way you nurture a ten-year-old will be different from the way you nurture a two-year-old. Similarly, the way you nurture Anabel, or Christie will be different from how you will nurture John or Peter. Each child and gender comes with its own demands.

WHAT ARE THE SPECIAL PHYSICAL BUILDING BLOCKS?

1. BONDING- A time to Serve & Connect (Age 0-4)
From age 0-4years, the child will literally need you for almost everything. He can do nothing to help himself. You breastfeed, cuddle, bath, clothe and take him to school or the Day-care Centre. Everything you do during this period must be centred on the child. You die to self to make him be. This gives room for complete bonding.

It is a time to connect and feel each other's warmth. The child should be given lots of time and attention. Constant cuddles from you help to develop a solid and stable bond. Keeping your baby in your arms helps the baby to feel secure and ultimately increases bonding.

For mothers, at this stage, you become a "servant" to the child, because the child "dictates" to you. He dictates when he wants to be fed... by a nagging cry. The Bible says, *"can a woman forget her sucking child that she should not have compassion on the son of her womb...?"* (Isaiah 49:15). This is unlikely, but not impossible. But for parents interested in nurturing their children to overcome in the journey of life, it is important not to abandon such needful responsibilities. You are a servant to your child at age 0- 4years. For instance, you cannot ignore a child that has just soiled his diaper. A responsible mother would naturally abandon whatever she is doing to attend to the baby, even while she is hungrily munching on a tantalizing snack! You are a servant!

The child determines where you go, what you wear, and what you eat (if you are breastfeeding). Good mum's commune with their children, while breastfeeding, and intercede in prayers for them.

You bond with the child to understand his/her feelings, temperament, and genetic make-up. It is a time of absolute commitment in bonding. This is the stage when the child recognises the voice and features of his parents. May your sheep hear your voice in Jesus Name .

2. LEADING- A time to Train and Instruct-(Age 5-14)

From this age, you are completely in charge. It is the time you instil your values in them. Proverbs 22:6 says, "Train up a child in the way he should go and when he is old he will not depart from it." You are no longer a servant to your child even though the bonding continues. You are a leader; A good leader with a goal in mind. You tell your child to sit and he sits. You don't ask a two-year-old to sit; you help him sit! The bonding you had established at ages 0-4 Years will be more reflective at this stage because the child would have grown to freely and gladly trust you.

Bonding had helped you train your sheep to hear your voice! Obedience to you as a leader becomes a matter of course. You are now a leader, an instructor. May your children obey your instructions in Jesus' name amen. Age 5-14 is the most critical stage of building character in a child because the child models after you.

Therefore, parents should be careful of their lifestyle. You are a leader, and for a leader to lead well, he has to lead himself first. The Bible says, "train" not "teach" or "lecture." While teaching is a one-off thing, training is a function of routine and pattern. Therefore, the Bible admonishes us to "train" the child.

Training involves a regular exercise, replete with spiritual, physical, emotional, and mental exertion. You "show and tell." You train him to wash, by washing with him, you train her to cook by cooking with her, you train him to eat by eating with him, and you teach him where to go and where not to go by going places with him. You lead by example. You are a role model and a mirror to your children. How are you leading your children?

This is the time parents should give their children the strong foundation needed to thrive and develop. As they grow into early teenage years, they want to become independent. Parents have the responsibility of changing from being a 'controller' to a 'consultant' at that stage.

Some parents teach their children to tell lies, by lying to their spouses. Rebecca made Jacob deceive his father, and the consequences were very grave. May your children not experience Jacob's trouble in Jesus Name Amen.

Parenting is a full-time job! Not by proxy, not by delegation. It is a dividend yielding enterprise, depending on your investments and you must pay your dues if you want your dividends to be succulent! Abraham paid his dues. (Genesis 18:19);

Today he is called the father of many nations. Eli failed in the field of godly parenting, and his lineage of priesthood was cut off The glory of God departed from his family line. (1 Samuel 2:30-34 & 4:22). The lamp of your glory will never be quenched in Jesus Name amen. The glory of your children shall burst forth like the sun in its full strength in Jesus Name Amen.

3. MENTORING- A time to guide, counsel and direct-(Ages 15-20). Becoming a parent of a teenager is like taking a long journey without a clue or guide. It takes tenacity and commitment from parents to help a teenage child navigate the demands of the teenage years.

Communicating with teenagers is often challenging. During the teenage years, the children are often uncommunicative. It is important to talk at their level. This is the age when the child is trying to take some life changing decisions. A teenager is a bundle of possibilities. He is at the "need to know" stage and with his rapidly maturing body and intellect he cannot wait to try new challenges. This is where you need to employ the "patience of Job" and be humble enough to come down to his level to understand his language. The rule is "first understand before you are understood." You are to guide and guard him prayerfully. Your spiritual antenna at this level must be very active. You mentor him, so he does not go into error. You don't impose your decisions on the child, but you help him take reasonable but rightful decisions e.g. career choices, academic choices, social choices, etc.

If your child says, "Dad I want to be a teacher." Don't shout him down and say: "No son, you must be an Engineer...Teachers are poorly paid!" Rather, as a godly parent, probe, to find out why he wants to be a teacher. Often, we force our children to study certain courses because of our ego. Because your son is good in physics and mathematics, you insist he must study Engineering, because it is prestigious to do so, irrespective of his passion or love for it.

But wise parents who want their children to overcome in the journey of life will inquire on their behalf in prayers like Rebecca did, and then help the child to focus on his goals and vision to achieve greatness.

Perhaps the child's destiny is in moulding lives, which he can only achieve as a teacher. That is why a lot of people are in the wrong professions today. They study medicine, instead of marketing, and end up treating patients like products! No wonder a lot of doctors lack humanity! Also, note that the "teen age" is the age of sexual exploration. Counsel them on sex and relationships. If you don't take time out to discuss this with them, they will learn from their friends, the internet, and books.

It is better to be their first teacher, mentor and counsellor, than for their friends to teach them. Their friends would teach them from their limited knowledge from other friends. But if you take the time to talk frankly with them about the consequences of immorality, they would not find it difficult to enter a covenant of purity with God before marriage.

4. FRIENDSHIP- A time to be pals and confidants -(Age 21-above). Here you become a friend to your child! He has transited into adulthood. He is a grown man/ woman ready for the world and ready to take responsibilities for his own actions! You don't lead a 21-year-old graduate; you befriend him. He is a man ready to test his wings and fly. You talk hard facts with him, man to man, woman to woman, and adult to adult. You win their continuous confidence and loyalty by doing this.

Sad but true, a lot of parents do not understand when a season is over! When your 25-year-old son calls you from work and says, "Dad I'll be going to Johannesburg first flight tomorrow," you don't start, by telling him, "Who asked you to?" He is a full-fledged adult now, capable of taking responsibilities for himself. You are his friend. You hold discussions with him. The days are gone when you yell at him or flog him. If you try that with a 20- year-old man or woman, they may overpower you with their youthful bones! The season is over!

Therefore, understand when a season is on, and when a season is over!

You don't befriend a child you are supposed to be leading neither do you serve a child you are supposed to be mentoring. Each block must be put in its place at the right time. This is how to develop character in the child. When you are sufficiently involved with the child, at each stage of his growth, you not only develop good character in the child, you will also help him to cultivate a good value system. The building blocks are the bones that hold the flesh in place. They are the pans that determine how the cake is shaped! They are the frame- work that shapes the character and the identity of the child, while the value system is the real substance and self-worth of the child. Good building blocks translate into good value systems. You cannot have one without having the other. The blocks are the forms while the values are the content. How then do you develop a good value system?

DEVELOP THE VALUE SYSTEM IN THE CHILD.

The value system of a child begins at home. It is a function of the child's nature and nurture. This is why it is important for parents to take their responsibilities seriously so they can have mighty arrows in their hands; **Steve Farrar** in his book, **"Finishing Strong"** says, *"To be raised in a home with true values of Christian culture is a great privilege."*

WHAT IS A VALUE SYSTEM?

A value system is a set of beliefs and behavioural patterns identified with a person over time. Values represent and reflect a person's sense of what is right and what is wrong. Therefore, it is important to inculcate the ethics of right, and wrong, into a child from the cradle.

What are those things you consider very important to you as parents? Whatever is important to you is what you will pass on to your children. Proverbs 1:10 says, *"My son, if sinners entice you consent thou not."*

If honesty is important to you, you will teach your child to return a borrowed pencil. If respect is important to you, you will teach your children to give up their seats for the elderly. The more values you teach your child, the more valuable he would become, and the more values people would place on him. It is my prayer that God will give you valuable children in Jesus Name. Amen.

Honesty, respect, faithfulness, reliability, love, teamwork, perseverance, etc., are great virtues that form a value system. These are the rules of moral conducts which you must inculcate into your children if you want them to be valuable in life.

But it doesn't just happen. They are built over time through purposeful nurturing, using the right building blocks, piece by piece *"...Precept upon precept; line upon line; here a little and there a little"* (Isaiah 28:10).

How do you make this happen? Let's look at the next sub-heading:

DEVELOPING A VALUE SYSTEM IN THE CHILD

According to Zorka Hereford, Author of "Essential life skills" a personal value system is a set of principles or ideals that drive and guide your behaviour. Your personal value system is the force behind your behaviour. These are rules or patterns of behaviour adopted or evolved by a person over time as a standard to guide his behaviour. It gives you structure and purpose, by helping you determine what is meaningful and important to you. Your value system helps you express who you are and what you stand for.

"Self-esteem is a major key to success in life. The development of a positive self-concept or healthy self-esteem is extremely important to the happiness and success of children and teenagers. Self-esteem is how we feel about ourselves, and our behaviour clearly reflects those feelings. For example, a child or teen with high self-esteem will be able to: act independently, assume responsibility and take pride in his accomplishments." https://childdevelopmentinfo.com/

If you as a parent do not have a value system, you cannot give it to your child. A child without a value system will stand for everything and invariably become the weakest link. May this not happen to your children in Jesus Name.

HOW THEN CAN YOU DEVELOP YOUR CHILD'S VALUE SYSTEM?

1. Define his spiritual commitment: These are the virtues that connect your child to God, which must first be seen in you. Lois' commitment to spiritual things reflected in Eunice her daughter and was then put into Timothy, her grandson. (2Timothy 1:5) You need to help your child develop a deep relationship with God.

Rick Warren, Author of 'The Purpose Driven Life,' says that *"...Real security is found only in that which cannot be taken away from you, and that is your relationship with God. Unless you lay it down and alienate it, no one can take it from you."*

Spiritual commitment, when fully practised, will give your child a sense of purpose beyond earthly existence and material needs. The child's life becomes focused when he knows his purpose. Involve your child in family prayers, encourage him to memorise short Bible verses relevant to his age, buy Christian literature for him and make yourself available and accessible for regular counselling and teaching of the Word of God. You must be available and ready to give him answers to seemingly unclear or disturbing questions. Don't be an absentee father or mother to your children.

Many parents are available but not accessible. They are around but not with their children. They shout the children down anytime they come to them for one need or the other. If you are available and accessible, your child will feel safe to confide in you. Susannah Wesley devoted her time to all her children. She devoted one hour a day to each child, teaching them biblical instructions. Her sons John and Charles became the founders of the Methodist church. Many of the hymns we sing in church today were written by Charles Wesley. Making your children committed to the things of God early in life, will not only give them real security in life's journey but will also guarantee unimaginable generational blessings. Today we talk about the Wesley brothers because of the excellent nurturing they received from their parents Susannah and John Wesley.

2. Develop the child's character and attitude. The Christian character is properly laid out in Galatians 5:22; (The fruits of the spirit). Teach him the Christian virtues of love, joy, peace, patience, gentleness, goodness, faith, meekness, and self-control. If he is not taught how to love, how will he respect people? If you teach him honesty and truth, peace will be with him always. The fruit of goodness and kindness give rise to family and social responsibility. Kindness activates selfless service. Without meekness, the child cannot be submissive or teachable, and without patience, he cannot have self-control, to help him relate to other people.

These are the Christian values that parents should inculcate into their children as they nurture them. When you develop these in the child, you are helping him define his self-worth and giving him a personal value system that will help him confront and overcome the challenges of life.

3. Develop the child's family values (i.e. relationships). This is the ability to love and care for those they are closely related to by blood or by affinity. Charity, they say, begins at home.

The way you treat your wife will determine how your son will treat his wife when he grows up. He knows no other way! The way you treat your guests and neighbours will determine how your children will treat people around them. Teach them to value family. Teach them to value human life. The Good Samaritan valued human and ready to give him answers to seemingly unclear or disturbing questions. Don't be an absentee father or mother to your children.

Many parents are available but not accessible. They are around but not with their children. They shout the children down anytime they come to them for one need or the other. If you are available and accessible, your child will feel safe to confide in you. Susannah Wesley devoted her time to all her children. She devoted one hour a day to each child, teaching them biblical instructions. Her sons John and Charles became the founders of the Methodist church. Many of the hymns we sing in church today were written by Charles Wesley. Making your children committed to the things of God early in life, will not only give them real security in life's journey but will also guarantee unimaginable generational blessings. Today we talk about the Wesley brothers because of the excellent nurturing they received from their parents Susannah and John Wesley.

2. Develop the child's character and attitude. The Christian character is properly laid out in Galatians 5:22; (The fruits of the spirit). Teach him the Christian virtues of love, joy, peace, patience, gentleness, goodness, faith, meekness, and self-control. If he is not taught how to love, how will he respect people? If you teach him honesty and truth, peace will be with him always. The fruit of goodness and kindness give rise to family and social responsibility. Kindness activates selfless service. Without meekness, the child cannot be submissive or teachable, and without patience, he cannot have self-control, to help him relate to other people.

These are the Christian values that parents should inculcate into their children as they nurture them. When you develop these in the child, you are helping him define his self-worth and giving him a personal value system that will help him confront and overcome the challenges of life.

3. Develop the child's family values (i.e. relationships). This is the ability to love and care for those they are closely related to by blood or by affinity. Charity, they say, begins at home.

The way you treat your wife will determine how your son will treat his wife when he grows up. He knows no other way! The way you treat your guests and neighbours will determine how your children will treat people around them. Teach them to value family. Teach them to value human life. The Good Samaritan valued human life that was why he did not need any sermon to help a dying victim of armed robbery. It is the lack of love for humanity that makes people get into public office and steal public funds.... Funds meant for schools and public utilities.

4. Develop his career values –This is the ability to express and put his skills to use, without hurting the people around him. It is the ability to express his gifts and use his talents and skills for the benefit of mankind. Whatever God has given to man, is not for the oppression of man but for the benefit of mankind. Mentor your child and teach him how to develop his life's goals for the interest of others.

5. Define relational boundaries-All things are good, but not all things are expedient. Creating boundaries for the child in the home will help the child respect other people's space. It is not everything you can afford that you give to your children. Teach your children the value of hard work. Teach them to value money. No matter how rich you are, let your child know that money is obtained by dint of hard work and God's mercies.

Some parents fly their children in first class to go to school. Such children can never know the value of hard work.

Some parents after toiling to send their children to school still spend their already drained energy looking for jobs for them. How will such children value the job? There is nothing wrong with putting a word or two for them, but carrying their C.V (curiculum vitae) from one company to the other while the children are gallivanting about with their friends is a tragedy! Define their boundaries. Let there be firm regulations in the home which the children should be made to adhere to. In some homes, no one stays out later than 8 p.m. Others would insist on knowing the parents of their children's friends before they can come to visit. These are boundaries that help the child to be principled in life and help him respect other people's lifestyles and principles.

However, recognise that your child is not perfect and indeed cannot be. If you the parents are not perfect why should your children be? Therefore, in developing their value systems, it is important to watch out for their weaknesses as well. Teach them how to deal with their weaknesses even as you are helping them develop their strengths. It is the balancing of these strengths against the weaknesses that will put your child in a good stead to overcome in the journey of life. **How do you balance their strengths against their weaknesses?**

BALANCING STRENGTHS AND WEAKNESSES

You don't judge a fish by its inability to climb a tree. Everyone is unique in his or her rights. Your children have been endowed with incredible abilities just like your neighbour's children. While utilising the building blocks for character development, also help the child discover his strengths and teach him how to deal with his weaknesses.

Not all children are good with calculations, and not all are expressive. The diversification of strengths and weaknesses if properly harnessed will make the world a better place. Apostle Paul says, *"Are all apostles? Are all Prophets? Are all teachers...? But earnestly desire the best gifts."* (1 Corinthians 12:29-31).

Teach your child to follow his dreams and help him confront his weaknesses if those weaknesses will impede on the actualization of his dreams.

How do you deal with your child's weaknesses?

1. Admit that the weaknesses truly exist. Do not ignore or deny the reality of his weaknesses. For instance, a child who cries easily when playing with his peers may indicate that he is very touchy and sensitive.

You complicate it, by always scolding him. What you should do is, build up his strength, by finding out why he was laughed at, and work out a solution. Eleanor Roosevelt said, "no one can make us feel inferior without our permission." However, don't be in denial, if the child is physically or mentally challenged. Some parents hide them at home, out of pain and hopelessness.

You will be doing the child the greatest disservice by doing this. Realise that you will not always be there for him, so help him to be independent, by taking him to a special needs school. Understand that the child has a right to his own life and with the aid of special skills he would be taught how to function in the normal world without having to depend on anybody. Be positive and be assured that something good *"will come out of his Nazareth."*

Nick Vujicic is a classic example. Here is a man born without arms and legs. But by the power of God and the unwavering support of his parents, he overcame that challenge. Today, he is an international presence, reaching out and inspiring able-bodied millions! For every disability, there is ability.

2. Find out what his/her natural strengths are. To find this out, you will need to probe more and understand the categories of the human temperaments and how they influence the character of people.

There are four basic human temperaments-

- The sanguine, (warm, lively and extroverted);
- The Choleric (Strong-willed, decisive and independent);
- The Melancholic (Analytical, self-sacrificing, and gifted);
- The Phlegmatic (Calm, easy going, peace loving).

Knowing your child's temperament will help you analyse his strengths and weaknesses, and then eventually help him find a balance.

3. Identify the weaknesses that are likely to interfere with his strengths. For instance, a Sanguine is very interactive and highly extroverted. His weakness may tend towards emotional instability and exaggerations. Such people are not likely to excel in mathematics. But looking at the long-term effect, there is no way mathematics will not interfere with the effectiveness of their future career choices e.g. Marketing, Sales Representatives, Events planning, etc. This is where parents need to strike a balance. The Sanguine is particularly energetic and boisterous in nature, and you need to apply a kinetic approach to making mathematics appealing and enjoyable to him.

4. Recognise that not all weaknesses need be addressed. The weaknesses that should be addressed are those which would interfere with the child's productivity or performances in class and in the future. If a child is not good at baseball, it should not be a cause for concern! There are other things he can excel at. You don't condemn a cow for its inability to eat meat! He is not wired for meat even though it has teeth.

5. Build his confidence by focusing on his comfort zone. Note that his area of interest is more important than his weaknesses. Don't force your child to study chemistry when he can excel in literature! Children never make great impact in their areas of weakness. So why waste your energy focusing on his weaknesses, when you can achieve more with him, by developing his strengths. As his confidence grows, he will be more willing to address his weaknesses if they impede on his overall performances.

6. Develop his strengths by encouraging hard work and commitment. It takes a determined person to achieve something tangible in life.

Teach him to be conscientious with his work in school and always teach him how to choose the road less travelled. Greatness in life is about hard work, determination, and commitment. It is not enough to just focus on his comfort zone and avoid his weaknesses and vice versa, as parents you must help your children work, and practice those strengths so they can gain a mastery of them.

The bottom line in balancing strengths and weaknesses is to help the child develop a character of peaceful co-existence in a world filled with men and women of great talents and gifts. This is how to overcome in the journey of life.

PRAYER POINTS

1. The anointing and the Power to train my children in the way of the Lord come upon my life in Jesus name.

2. You my children (mention their names), you will not harvest any bad character in my life line, in Jesus name.

3. Oh Lord give me divine strength and courage to support my children in the right things which seem unpopular with the world.

4. As the rod of Aaron stood out and budded amongst the rods of the Levites, Oh Lord arise and let my children be singled out from the crowd for greatness. Nothing will make them get lost in the crowd.

5. Jacob had twelve children, and each one of them was great in his own right. You my children (names), I speak greatness into your lives. You shall accomplish your divine purpose. You shall never be missing among great people in Jesus name.

6. The Godly character of hospitality and kindness that promoted the destiny of Rebecca, come upon my children's lives for destiny elevation, in Jesus name.

7. No matter how many you are, you shall stand out. You shall be independent of each other; you shall not beg from each other in Jesus name.

CHAPTER FIVE

The Place Of Prayer And Spirituality

Prayer has been defined as a supplication, entreaty or appeal to God. According to Dr. D.K. Olukoya, General Overseer, Mountain of Fire and Miracles Ministries, prayer is "the rail on which the train of God's power moves.... It is the insistence that the will of God be done on earth as it is in heaven.... It is the deepest expression of the soul and the most potent force in the universe."

The greatest weapon in the hands of parents to fight the battles confronting their children's destiny is prayer. Lamentations 2:19 says: *"Arise cry out in the night: in the beginning of the watches pour out thine heart like water before the face of the Lord: lift up thine hands towards Him for the life of thine young children that faint for hunger in the top of every street."* (emphasis mine). It takes groaning tears to produce a child of destiny!

GOD'S PATTERN FOR PARENTAL NURTURING

John Mason, Author of *"An Enemy called Average,"* says "the greatest tragedy is not unanswered prayers, but unoffered prayers..." You may miss it in sermons, you may miss it in praise and worship, but you can never miss it in prayers.

Prayer succeeds where all else fail!

Good parents mould their children's destiny on their knees and define their pathways through importunate prevailing prayers. This means that at every stage of parenting, you must tirelessly commit your children to God. Pray them out of evil and unprofitable relationships and pray them into their original glories and destinies. Nothing can stand the fire of prayer! You are a covering over them. Your prayer is a covering to shield them from the fiery darts of wickedness.

Bill Graham's mother, Morrow Coffey Graham, once said in an interview with Christianity Today "...I pray without ceasing for Billy." And she became the mother of one of the world's greatest evangelists. Therefore, as parents, you must stand firmly behind your children in prayers. Now let's look at how you can be a covering to your children.

BE A GOOD COVERING

To be a good covering, you should do all you can to ensure that no harm comes to your children, physically and spiritually. God has put you there as a covering over your children, and so, they must enjoy your complete protection. Sarah is a classic example. The woman she chose to share her husband's bed with her, began to mock her and despise her only son Isaac. What did she do? She didn't fold her arms and leave her son to the mercy of a destiny destroyer! She said to Abraham, her husband, "Cast out this bondwoman and her son: for the son of this bondwoman shall not be heir with my son, even Isaac." Though Abraham was very much displeased, God backed Sarah up and told him, *"hearken unto her voice."* Dear parents, don't be too naïve or too emotional to take firm decisions to protect your children. Nobody can love your children more than you.

Like a seed that needs the covering of the soil to germinate, spiritual covering of parents is a necessity for the development of their children's character. The Bible says, *"...And it came to pass as he sowed, some fell by the way side, and the fowls of the air came and devoured it up....And others fell on good ground and did yield fruits that sprang up and increased..."* (Mark 4:4-8).

As illustrated by the parable of the sower, the seeds that fell on the way side were easily devoured because of lack of covering by the soil.

Apart from protection, the soil provides the right conditions for a seed to grow. In like manner, the self-esteem of a child can be battered or enhanced depending on the atmosphere of protection created and given by the parents. Show me a child with a strong personality, and I will show you one with a solid spiritual covering.

A godly parent would willingly give up her rights and comfort for the safety and welfare of her children. King Solomon was about to divide a living child in two, to share among the two women claiming to be his mother. The real mother who understood the power of 'covering' willingly gave up her right so that her son would live and not die. The Bible says, "...*For her bowels yearned upon her son...*"

The mother is the spiritual mother-hen of the home. She is a natural fighter. As a mother, you are a roof and an umbrella over your children. Jochebed refused to surrender her son Moses to the evil sword of Pharaoh. Like Jochebed and Hannah, I counsel you to take your children to the Lord for covering...

Likewise, you fathers. You are the spiritual head of the home. You must learn how to lead the family altar. Elkanah led the family to Shiloh year in year out. The Bible records that, "when the time was that Elkanah offered, he gave to Peninnah, his wife and all her sons and daughters, portions: But unto Hannah, "he gave a worthy portion;" (1Samuel 1:4-5). Why? He did this to protect her, and to balance the marital equation, so that it would not be said that she was deprived, for lack of children.

Elkanah was a responsible father and husband, and so was Job. The Bible says that after every feast organised by his children, Job would summon them together and sanctify them. Getting up early in the morning, he would offer a burnt offering for each of them, lest they become desecrated. This was a regular practice in the house of Job.

Let nothing be too small and inconsequential or too great and complicated to table before God.

Parents should prayerfully guide and guard their children at every stage of their development. Spirituality gives direction. It is the compass that guides the children to destiny. To do this effectively, you must always partner with the Holy Spirit.

You must also take care of your umbrella of covering, so it doesn't have holes. Sin, worldliness, and careless living are all elements that puncture holes in the umbrella of protection. This generally inhibits growth and development.

HOW CAN YOU BE A COVERING TO YOUR CHILDREN?

1. Secure their souls in Christ. This is the greatest and most superior covering of all. But to do this, you must have secured yours too. Or else how can the blind protect or lead the blind? (Matthew 15:14). You secure them in Christ by leading them to Christ and making them say the sinner's prayers.

2. Always pray for them and with them. However, it is not enough to pray for them. You must always pray with them and teach them how to pray. Let them be familiar with the rhythm of your prayers. By praying with them, you are teaching them how to fight for themselves and not always dependent on their parents. Therefore, whatever challenges they face they would be able to confront them in prayers, with the mind-set of "oh this was how my parents handled it in prayers."

By praying with them, you are teaching them how to overcome in the journey of life. Salvation is personal. It is amazing and indeed disturbing when parents, especially mothers come to church regularly with the photographs of their children, who perhaps are still snoring in bed or dancing away their lives in nightclubs. Where are the children? If you had taken time to nurture them from the cradle, you wouldn't need to persuade them to come with you to church. It would be a matter of course.

3. Be watchful and involved. Always watch out for dangerous signals and have the courage to correct them. This was perhaps where Manoah and his wife missed it in the life of their son, Samson. Every vice must be identified early and promptly dealt with. Know the friends your children hang out with and know their parents so as to have a fair assessment of the kind of home such friends come from.

The Bible says evil communication corrupt good minds. Therefore, no matter how well you try to nurture your children if you are not watchful, and you fail to involve yourself in their activities and lifestyle they would be corrupted by their friends.

4. Always arm yourself with spiritual weapons. Prayer is the greatest weapon in time of war. There are different kinds of prayer which parents can use.

To be an effective covering over your children, you must learn how to pray *warfare prayers* and *prayers of enquiry*.

Rebecca prayed enquiry prayers when her pregnancy was challenged. She wondered ... *"If it be so, why is it thus with me?"* And the Bible says she went to enquire of the Lord. Then God revealed to her that *"two nations"* were in her womb! (Genesis 25:22-23).

Beloved parents, until you pray enquiry prayers, you may not receive revelation. David also enquired from God if he should pursue and overtake. He also prayed to God using great spiritual weapons. The Bible says we should not be ignorant of the devices of the enemies. For you to be an effective covering over your children, you must understand how to use spiritual weapons and USE THEM EFFECTIVELY. The Bible says" the weapons of our warfare are not carnal but mighty through God, to the pulling down of strongholds". (2Corinthians 10:4).

These weapons have been given to us as Christians to make us victorious in the battlefield of life. In ensuring that your children overcome in the journey of life you must be aware of the devices of the enemies and take advantage of the available spiritual weapons, God has provided through Jesus Christ. What are these weapons?

a. The Blood of Jesus
b. The Word of God
c. The Name of Jesus
d. The Fire of God

Use these weapons against 'destiny quenchers' and 'problem activators' troubling the progress of your children. A young undergraduate was engaged to a guy who was lying to her that he was a master's degree holder, whereas he didn't go beyond secondary school. He could pull through with the deception because he could speak impeccable English. The problem was not his education but his deceptive character. Without saying a word, her mother went on her knees and scattered the relationship using the spiritual weapons at her disposal. Today the lady is happily married to a lecturer. Her mother won without words! You are a covering over your children.

Sadly, some parents are still playing hide and seek with the destiny of their children. Without prayer, you can never have spiritual boldness and victory. Elizabeth understood the implication of allowing the tradition of men, circumstances of life, man-made establishments or institutions to define the destiny of her son, John the Baptist. This was perhaps where Jabez's mother missed it. It was the power of prayer that gave Elizabeth the spiritual boldness to say, "NOT SO" to family traditions contrary to God's will for her son. (Luke 1:59-64) My prayer for you is that the enemy will not rejoice over your ignorance in Jesus Name. As parents, always be prepared to fight the good fight of faith on behalf of your children.

SPIRITUALITY AS A COMPASS FOR DIVINE DIRECTION

Prayers help to give divine direction and a proper course in life's journey. Prayer strengthens and toughens the children and makes them develop a remarkable courage for life's endeavours. Psalm 119:105 says, *"the word of God is a lamp unto my feet and a light unto my path."* Proverbs 16:9 also says *"...A man's heart deviseth his ways, but God directeth his steps."* Spirituality gives direction. If a child is grounded in the word of God, it will be difficult for that child to stumble or miss it. This is why you must take your children's spiritual lives seriously.

Both Old and New Testaments are very clear about communicating spiritual truth to the children.

"Hear, O Israel: The LORD our God, the LORD is one. Love the LORD your God with all your heart and with all your soul and with all your strength. These commandments that I give you today are to be upon your hearts. Impress them on your children. Talk about them when you sit at home and when you walk along the road, when you lie down and when you get up. Tie them as symbols on your hands and bind them on your foreheads. Write them on the doorframes of your houses and on your gates." (Deuteronomy 6:4-9)

Jesus called the children to him and said, "Let the little children come to me, and do not hinder them, for the kingdom of God belongs to such as these. I tell you the truth anyone who will not receive the kingdom of God like a little child will never enter it." (Luke 18:16-17)

Conversations about God should be regular just as other subjects of discussion in the family. Children should see parents pray about other issues of life, give thanks to God for His provisions and accept God's leading in every decision making.

I pray that in the journey of life, your children will not go astray in Jesus Name.

PRAYER POINTS

1. Oh Lord, my Father give me oil in my lamp and keep me burning day and night in prayers before you in Jesus Name.

2. The anointing to pray, and to prevail in prayers let it come to me like Hannah in the Name of Jesus.

3. In the battlefield of life, my children will not become casualties. They shall not be victims of other people's errors and negligence in Jesus Name.

4. The umbrella of covering over my children, will not be torn, it you will not leak, and it will not fold up suddenly in Jesus Name.

5. I decree that my children will not make me throw away my Bible in Jesus Name.

6. Oh Lord convert my point of shame and ridicule over my children to points of glory and honour in Jesus Name.

7. Oh Lord replace my tears and groaning for my children with endless joy and laughter in Jesus Name.

CHAPTER SIX

The Relevance Of Vision

Proverbs 29:18 says: "where there is no vision the people perish: but he that keepeth the law happy is he." Vision is the image of the future. Vision is your tomorrow. It is the big picture of how one perceives his future.

WHAT IS THE RELEVANCE OF VISION?

Here we are looking at the importance or significance of helping your child create a vision for him/her. The relevance of vision cannot be over emphasised.

1.) Vision makes destiny happen. Once you can imagine it, you will achieve it, if you run with it. The people of Babel came together, with the purpose of building a city and a tower *"whose top may reach up to heaven and God said, "...nothing will be restrained from them which they have imagined doing."* **(Genesis 11:6).**

Although God scattered it, it was not because of their vision, but because of their motives.

2. Vision is the big picture of what you want to achieve. It is the ultimate picture of how the future will look like. Having the picture or the goal in your mind makes you a goal getter. Peter Drucker, was reported (by Brian Tracy) to have said that even when a business is starting out on a kitchen table if the business dreams of world leadership, it will end up a huge success.

3. Vision brings about creativity. An idle mind is the devil's workshop. Ben Carson says, "The regular exercise of your imagination will enhance your natural creativity." With vision, the mind becomes purposeful and actively concerned with how to accomplish the set goals. With vision, new ideas are generated. And you create events to make it happen.

4. Vision brings transformation (i.e. change in attitude, character, and mind-set.) When a child knows his goal in life, his language and attitude. His vision will inspire action. His vision will develop his mind and give him a new approach to issues. It will propel him to give his best. It will drift him towards eagles and move him away from chickens.

5. Vision encourages hard work. A man without a vision is a lazy man. If a child's vision is to become a dentist, he would naturally strive to obtain excellent results in all his science subjects to achieve his dreams.

6. Vision is a resource to other people's visions. Romans 8:19 says: "the earnest expectation of the creature waiteth for the manifestation of the sons of God." The world is waiting with bated breath for your child's manifestation. Until he manifests, people around him may not manifest. This is because in the journey of life he would meet people whose destinies are attached to his. He becomes a role model to other aspiring colleagues. That is why you must help him to achieve destiny.

The reason why a lot of young men and women are visionless is primarily because of their faulty foundations in both nature and nurture. A good parent should help the child develop his vision and keep him focused until it is actualized and self-discovery is the gateway to actualizing a vision.

LEADING THE JOURNEY TO SELF – DISCOVERY

Self-Discovery is the realisation of oneself. It is finding your relevance and purpose in life; it is knowing what God had at the back of His mind before creating you. It is one thing to know who you are (self-identity) and it is another thing to know why you are here (self-discovery). Some children discover themselves very early in life while some do so at a later age. Some don't at all or do so when the vision is no longer relevant to their existence. What is the use of fried chicken in the mouth of a 95-year-old man! For a child not to achieve his full potential, it is important that he is properly guided by his parents.

In the previous chapter, we talked about the building blocks, part of which is about the parent becoming a leader to the child when he/she is between the ages of 5-14. Our destiny is a function of time. This is the age when the child is trying to discover his strengths and purpose, and he would need your help.

HOW DO YOU LEAD YOUR CHILD IN THE JOURNEY TO SELF-DISCOVERY?

1. Understand his dominant temperament. In chapter three, I touched briefly on temperaments, and I said every person is an embodiment of the four basic human temperaments i.e. sanguine, choleric, phlegmatic and melancholy. Please be aware that there is a remnant of each temperament, in every individual, and there is also a predominance of each in every individual. You are expected to understand your child's temperament, by studying him/her over time. Hence, bonding with your child is important. If you don't bond, you would not know. You study your child through bonding, leading, and mentoring according to their ages as discussed in chapter three until you understand his/her strengths.

A child who can pick out the minutest details in every issue is likely to be a choleric and therefore would be comfortable with science and calculations. A child who loves people celebrates friendship and is generally outgoing is likely to be a sanguine and therefore more comfortable with the Arts and humanities and may want to be a lawyer, an administrator or a sales representative, etc. It is important as a parent to understand their disposition in order to prayerfully guide them.

2. Probe into him to bring out the best in him. It is not enough to understand his temperament. Probe the child to be sure he has a passion for the vision.

Are you sure he is not copying someone else's vision? How do you probe? Find out what he does with joy and ease. Find out what he is angry about, that he feels like changing. What does he do with little or no supervision? What value is he adding to people around him, that brings him commendation, or make people glorify God because of him? These are likely pointers to self-discovery. And self-discovery is the gateway to destiny. As a parent, God wants you to mentor him, to achieve more.

3. Give him all the encouragement he needs. In the journey to self-discovery, the one person, your child, must not fail to see when he looks back, is you. He will look back; for fear, for doubt, and of course for reassurance. He needs to know he is on track. You are the one person he must not fail to see, when he looks back! For every person, there is a "frightened child within." The one person Albert Einstein did not fail to see when he 'looked back' was his mum, Pauline Einstein. She believed in him even when his entire school had written him off, as a slow learner-a dyslexic. But Pauline stood by him and encouraged him to "walk on waters."

Therefore, when your child does not seem to have a vision, or it appears that things are not going as expected with your child; the answer is **NEVER GIVE UP**.

Never give up! The Bible says, "there is hope for a tree cut down...At the scent of water, it will bud and bring forth branches like a plant..." (Job: 14:8-9). There is always a way out. There is a light at the end of every tunnel.

John Mason the Author of "The Enemy called average" said, "... The divine direction is not seen but heard...." Teach the child to train the ears of his mind diligently so he can hear like Samuel heard God. The word, "I can't" has hindered many colourful destinies. The Bible says we can do all things through Christ that strengthens us. Teach your child to look up to Jesus and not the waters. If his eyes are fixated on Jesus, he will walk on the waters!

As a parent, you must not give up on any child for any reason. Present challenges of life must not make you throw in the towel on any child. God is able, and with Him all things are possible. (Luke 1:37).

You must understand that children are like fruits. They come in different shapes, sizes and colours.

While some are like coconuts that are very tough to break, some are like grapes both soft inside and outside. This is part of the mystery of life, and as the Bible rightly puts it, we only know in parts as human beings.

Recently, I was privileged to teach a set of identical twins, who had completely opposite personalities; while one of them is an introvert and gifted in mathematics, the other is an extrovert and not very strong in mathematics. Also, while the first is better behaved, the other is a cause for concern to her mother. This became a concern to me as there is no scientific explanation for this disparity. This rein¬forces the danger of comparing children.

As parents, you must understand that children are unique and each child should be treated individually with respect and love.

Never give up on your child even if everything about him is singing a negative tune. In every disability, there is an ability that brings glory to God. You are called to be your children's cheerleader!

There are organisations, government agencies willing offer help. Accept offers of help instead of giving up. Don't be too down and proud to accept offers extended to you.

Again, never give up on yourself. If you have missed it in your time, that is not an excuse to allow your children to become failures. Your children will reach their destiny in life in Jesus name amen. Learn from King David; Even though he was disqualified by God not to build the temple in Jerusalem, that didn't stop him from encouraging his son Solomon from building the temple. What you are unable to achieve in your lifetime your children will achieve and exceed it in Jesus Name. Josiah's father Amon could not offer much to him as a father, but the Bible says he (Josiah) *"...did that which was right in the sight of the Lord...and turned not aside to the right hand or to the left"* (2Kings: 22:2). You need to keep on encouraging them. Never give up!

One way to encourage them is by building up their capacity to develop a 'single eye' on their dreams and visions.

UNDERSTANDING THE SINGLE EYE THEORY

For destiny actualization, you must teach your child the 'single eye' theory. The Bible says, *"...if your eye is single your whole body will be full of light...But if your eye is evil your whole body will be full of darkness"* (Matthew 6:22).

The single eye theory is the doctrine of absolute focus. Proverbs 4:25-27 says, *"Let thine eyes look right on and let thine eyelids look straight before thee...turn not to the right hand nor to the left."* The Bible also says that whatever your hands find to do, do it with all thy strength.

HOW DOES YOUR CHILD DEVELOP A SINGLE EYE ON HIS VISION?

1. Hard work, determination and focus: Hard work and focused determination can never be overemphasised. Teach your child to give full attention to his vision. Focus is the ability to develop a single-minded approach to an issue. James 1:8 says, *"a double minded man is unstable in all his ways."* Therefore focus makes the child stable and helps activate destiny. Also, note that there is dignity in labour. It is funny how people pray so hard and work so little. This is irresponsible faith! It is true that God owns the yam and gives the knife. But He will not cook it and put it in your mouth! Let your children understand the importance of hard work. To excel in life, they need to work hard.

THE RELEVANCE OF VISION

2. Forget the past. The past can either be a positive or negative experience. The positive ones are testimonies which should reasonably boost better productivity, while the negative ones kill productivity. However, the danger of dwelling too much on yesterday's success is that you will become too complacent. You will become a man/woman of yesterday-a champion in history, while you yet live! God forbid! If all a man can boast of is what he had achieved yesterday, he will become visionless. The anointing of yesterday can never be sufficient for today.

Conversely, when a person keeps dwelling on his past mistakes and failures, he prepares the ground for greater failure. When you keep looking back, you stumble. When does a driver keep considering the rear mirror what happens? CRASH...BOOM!! Is what he hears, God forbid! Therefore, teach your children to put the past where it belongs. There is always room for improvement.

3. Avoid distractions. Distractions take the child away from the vision. And when the vision stops receiving attention it dies. Attention to a vision is like water on a plant. Job 14:7 says. *"There is hope of a tree if it is cut down that it will sprout again...through the scent of water it will bud..."*

Train your child to always give attention to his goals. Social media is the greatest distraction if not well managed.

4. Commit the child to constant improvement. It is not enough to be the best in his class. Teach him to beat the best! Let him break his own record if need be. There is always room for improvement.

5. Train your child to cultivate a healthy and positive mind-set. Proverbs 23:7 says *"For as a man thinketh in his heart so is he."* A positive mind-set always secure victory. David confronted Goliath with a positive mind-set even when his own brothers discouraged him. Jehoshaphat was positive on the way to battle even when everything around them appeared gloomy. They received victory in the end. Conversely, ten out of the twelve spies spoke in negative terms. They compared themselves to grasshoppers as against the inhabitants of the land they had gone to spy, and indeed they were destroyed like grasshoppers!

Victory starts from the heart. The power to overcome in the journey of life begins from the heart. If the mind-set is not renewed, victory becomes a mirage.

PRAYER POINTS

1. Oh Lord, my Father, rearrange the thinking pattern of my children for greatness in Jesus Name.

2. The vision that will make my children relevant and excel in life, Oh Lord my Father give it to them in the Name of Jesus.

3. Oh Lord, my Father, open the eyes of my children's heart to see where You have destined them to be in life and empower them to get there, in Jesus Name.

4. Father Lord I pray, remove my children from the pathway of vision killers and destiny wasters, in Jesus Name

5. Anointing for unusual favour, fall upon my children anywhere they go in life in Jesus Name.

6. Jehovah Jireh, I pray, let the gifts of my children create vacancies for them in palaces and uncommon establishments. Let them arise as answers to people's questions like Daniel in the land of Babylon in Jesus Name.

7. John the Baptist preached in the wilderness without a cathedral, yet great men of renown sought to hear from him. You my children, no matter where you are located, you shall be highly sought after by men and women all over the world in Jesus Name.

CHAPTER SEVEN

The Right Counsel
(Avoiding the seat of the ungodly)

You cannot use wood to sharpen a cutlass. Therefore, no matter how wise a child is, or how well he was brought up, if he chooses to sit with fools he will end up a fool. This is because "iron sharpens iron." A preacher once said that: "... If he associates himself with those disconnected from heaven, he will eventually lose his connection to heaven..."

Rehoboam, the son of King Solomon, the wisest king in Israel, sat in the seat of the ungodly. The people of Israel came on an appeal mission to him, pleading that their burdens be lightened. Rather than rely on the counsel of the elders, he sought counsel with his friends who taught him what to say to the oppressed. And this was what he said: "...My father chastised you with whips, but I will chastise you with scorpions" And what was the consequence of this unguarded utterance? His kingdom was divided!

He lost ten tribes of Israel to Jeroboam and retained only two. This is what wrong counselling can do to a glorious destiny. I pray for you; may your children never sit in the seat of the ungodly in Jesus Name.

"There is a way which seemeth right unto a man, but the end thereof are the ways of death." (Proverbs 14:12). It was the evil counsel from Jonadab that influenced David's son Amnon to rape his own sister Tamar, and death was the result. (2Samuel 13) Likewise Samson; He sat with Delilah and ended up dying with his enemies. The Bible says where no counsel is the people fall. But in the multitude of counsellors, there is safety.

Where are your children now? Do you know who they are hanging out with? As parents, you have the primary responsibility to train them to avoid the seat of the ungodly.

HOW DO YOU AVOID THE SEAT OF THE UNGODLY?

1. Avoid negative peer pressures. Ben Carson, a renowned neurosurgeon, defines "Peers" as *"People who Encourage Errors, Rudeness and Stupidity"* and that is the summation of the pressure they exert on each other!

The Bible records that Rehoboam forsook the counsel of the old men and took the counsel of the young men who had "grown up with him. And these young men put the spirit of error, rudeness and stupidity into him. For your children to be what God wants them to be there are people they must separate themselves from. You must insist on not only knowing the friends your children hang out with, but also know their parents. At least have a fair idea of who they are and where they are coming from.

2. Keep your children away from useless socializing. Friendship is by choice not by force. A child would eventually resemble the people he spends his time with. Always ask your child, what value an outing will add to his life before letting him go. If a friend is not adding any value to your child, prayerfully separate them.

3. Freedom is conditional, not absolute. Even in the Garden of Eden, freedom was not absolute. Adam was given dominion. But his dominion stopped where the tree of life began! Always set ground rules for your children, so they know their limits, especially regarding social activities. It is not enough to let them go out with their friends, but you must always insist they come home at a particular time.

This will help the child guard his liberty when he grows up. The reason why many wives are in sorrow today is that of the unlimited freedom exercised by their husbands in social outings. They go clubbing with friends and never have the mind of returning home until their friends bring them back drunk. Many men are in trouble today because of the negative influences of their wives' 'friends. All these are rooted in faulty parenting.

4. Teach them the power to say "No." Beloved parents the word "No" is an anointed word. "No" is the foundation of positive choices and actions. A child taught to say "No" very early in life, will move very far in life. The Bible says all things are good, but not all things are expedient. The power to say no will help the child avoid serious mistakes in life. Teach him to say "NO!" to alcohol!, "No" to drugs, to fornication, laziness, worldliness and the likes.

OVERCOMING FAMILY COMPARISONS

The Bible says comparing themselves to themselves, they are not wise. Family comparison is the bane of African civilization. This is often rooted in envy and wickedness. No one wants the other man's children in the family to rise above his own. Micah 7:6 says, *"...A man's enemies are members of his own household."*

WHY DO YOU NEED TO OVERCOME FAMILY COMPARISON?

As a parent, you need to shield your children from both internal and external forces. God has made you a covering over them, and you must rise and stand in the gap, as a great covering, so you don't leave them at the mercy of wicked people.

Many times, parents announce their children's glories even before they begin to shine. Why do you need to announce to the world that your son has gained admission into the university? Micah 7:5-6 says, *"Trust ye not a friend; put ye not confidence in a guide: keep the doors of thy mouth from her that lieth in thy bosom. For the son dishonoureth the father, the daughter riseth up against her mother, the daughter in- law against her mother in-law; a man's enemies are members of his household."* There is a proverb commonly used in the south-west of Nigeria which says, *"The termite eating the vegetable, is resident in the vegetable."*

Evil comparison brings nothing but trouble. It brings unfulfilled dreams and visions, and it wastes destinies.

HOW DO YOU OVERCOME EVIL COMPARISON?

1. Have secretive wisdom. Proverbs 29:11 says, *"A fool uttereth all his mind but a wise man keepeth it in till afterwards."* Nobody can quote silence! Keep your family affairs private. Whether your children are meeting up to your expectation or not, tell it to God and not to family members. Some parents are fond of revealing family matters or family decisions to other members of the larger families, perhaps for want of solution or out of exasperation or even excitement. This is very wrong. All you are doing is exposing your children to danger.

King Saul understood the power of secretive wisdom. After he was anointed King by Samuel, the Bible says, "So Saul said to his uncle *'He told us plainly that the donkeys had been found'* But about the matter of the kingdom, he did not tell him what Samuel had said." (1Samuel 10:16).

I heard the story of a father who kept praising his daughter and telling his uncle how he would put her in Corona school (one of the top schools in Nigeria) when she grew up. The man eventually lost his job in the bank and survival became a struggle. He managed to enrol the child at a substandard roadside school! Not too long after this, the Uncle went visiting and saw the children preparing for school and then asked in mockery, "I thought you said your children would attend Corona!" It is important to have secretive wisdom, so you don't expose yourselves and your children to danger and ridicule. 2 Samuel 1:20 says *"Tell it not in Gath, publish it not in the streets of Askelon; lest the daughters of the Philistines rejoice, lest the daughters of the uncircumcised triumph."* May you not be a victim of family mockery in Jesus Name.

Testimonies are good, but you must share it with wisdom. Tell the testimony of the birth of the child and not the testimony of the pregnancy. Tell the testimony of the house you have built/bought, and not the land/mortgage you have acquired to build or buy the house. Beloved parents, wisdom is profitable for direction. Show off is the grandfather of evil arrows! God will give you understanding in Jesus Name.

2. Every marriage must establish its own home. (Unguarded incursion breeds unhealthy interactions.) Some husbands have converted their house into a charity home! All roads lead to their homes. It is good to help people, but you must do it with wisdom.

GOD'S PATTERN FOR PARENTAL NURTURING

Dear parents, you do not have to bring a person to your house to assist him. You will be exposing your spouse and children to untold danger. The person you bring to the house has no stake at all. If anything happens, he will walk away. At best, he will be your personal broadcast station and will announce your 'failures' to the world.

Wisdom demands that you maintain your own home with your wife and children to avoid undue and unholy comparison.

3. Be careful where you go, to seek for help. There is nothing wrong in seeking help but be mindful where and how you get the help. Women are more vulnerable in this regard. They expose their husbands' weaknesses to too many unfriendly friends. Out of 100 things, they are fond of focusing on the one thing their husbands failed to do rather than the 99 things their husbands have done.

Marriage is a function of two imperfect people coming together. Please be careful where you go to for help. If Sisera had known Jael's intention, he would not have gone into her tent to rest when Deborah's army pursued him.

4. Guard the door of your mouth: A lot of parents suffer from verbal diarrhoea! It is not everything that God reveals to you about your children that you must say.

> *"In the multitudes of words there wanteth not sin: but he that refraineth his lips is wise."* Proverbs 10:19

Too much talk makes a person lose control, and a lot is revealed in the multitude of words, which can never be taken back.

5. Pray for discernment: Discernment will keep the mouth in check and the mind connected to heaven at every conversation. When the mind is connected to heaven, you will know how to speak in season and out of season. Proverbs 13:3 says: "He that keepeth his mouth keepeth his life; but he that openeth wide his lips shall have destruction."

OVERCOMING ENVIRONMENTAL CHALLENGES

The environment you live plays a major role in child nurturing. That is why if you give birth to a set of twins and put one in the village and the other in the city they invariably behave like distant relatives. Your environment defines you, just as your location defines your allocation.

We can't all live in a plush environment. Your environment most times is determined by your financial capacity. However, a child of God must take charge of his environment. God created you to have dominion.

So, wherever you find yourself whether poor or plush, have dominion. When you have dominion, you don't let your environment define you; you define your environment.

Decide to raise your children differently despite the environment you find yourself. God will relocate you if He sees how truthful and determined you are.

PRAYER POINTS

1. Oh God arise and raise a mountain between my mouth and my heart so that I will not endanger the destiny of my children with unguarded words, in Jesus Name.

2. You my children I separate you from unfriendly friends and I raise a dividing wall between you and them in Jesus Name.

3. It is written *"Associate yourselves o ye people and ye shall be broken in pieces...take counsel together, and it shall come to nought. Speak the word, and it shall not stand: for God is with us"* (Isaiah 8:9).

I stand in the authority of these words, and I scatter unto desolation any evil camp, evil association and useless friends luring or planning to initiate my children into cultism, evil gang ups and valueless associations, in Jesus Name.

4. I frustrate every wicked family counsel, and every demonic manipulation, camouflaging as counsel against the peace and progress of my children. Thus, says the Lord "It shall not stand neither shall it come to pass" (Isaiah 7:7) I decree that you the rod of evil family rivalry and competition raised against my children will not prosper. Be rendered impotent in the Name of Jesus Amen.

5. Oh, Lord, I pray in whatever company my children find themselves, whether in school or at work, give them the power to say "No" to standards contrary to your words. Give them a mouth and wisdom which their adversaries cannot gainsay in the Name of Jesus. (Luke 21:15)

6. You my children (mention their names) where ever you face in life, north, west, east and south, Jehovah the God of Jeshurun will go before you and make way for you in Jesus Name.

7. You my children you will not be a bad example to avoid but a good example to emulate in Jesus Name.

CHAPTER EIGHT

Leaving A Good Legacy

There are three seasons to parenting. Season one is the period when you take care of the child. Season two is the period you let the child take care of himself/herself, and season three is the period when the child takes care of both himself and you. Sad but true, season three is determined by what you achieved in season one. And this season will eventually out live you if you put enough into parenting.

Season three is a time to harvest. It is a time to rest. What you sow in season one will translate into harvest in the third season of parenting. This will eventually become the legacy you are leaving behind.

WHAT WILL YOU BE REMEMBERED FOR?

No man is remembered for what he receives but for what he gives. Proverbs 13:22 says, *"A good man leaves an inheritance for his children's children..."* Inheritance is not about physical possessions. In fact, a man is not remembered by the number of houses, or cars he acquired, but by the number of lives he touched.

What memories of yourself are you leaving behind? When your name resonates in the heart of people, what will it evoke? When we hear of Pharaoh today what comes to mind is 'a satanic task master.' Herod reminds us of 'the killer of good things in their infancy.' Ruth is remembered as a woman of deep rooted loyalty and total allegiance to God.

Today whenever the name of Pastor E.A. Adeboye is mentioned, meekness, humility, faithfulness and unfeigned love for God and for Kingdom service are evoked. How will your children remember you? What will the world recall about you? To be remembered you must have given all or any of the following:

1. A GOOD NAME: Proverbs 22:1 says, *"A good name is to be chosen rather than great riches, loving favour rather than silver and gold."* Protect your name. Value what you stand for, and reproduce it in the lives of your children. Don't just stand for anything. For instance: if it is hard work that you choose to stand for, then stand for it. Make sure you let your children understand that hard work does not kill. It is poverty that kills. Teach them to maintain unashamed integrity in the dignity of labour.

2. SELFLESS SERVICE: Do things for the interest and the good of all and not just for the good of your children alone. Let humanity benefit from you. Life is best lived in service to others. In south west Nigeria the sage, Obafemi Awolowo is remembered today for the free education his government gave to the people.

3. SELF-SACRIFICE: Go the extra mile for people. The good you do for them will eventually speak for you and raise a voice for your children and family members where their voices cannot be heard.

Jonathan sacrificed his throne for David on the altar of friendship, and this self-sacrifice raised a voice for Mephibosheth, a lame man condemned in the land of Lodebar.

I pray for you that your good works will raise a voice for your children in Jesus Name.

4. BE RELEVANT TO YOUR COMMUNITY: In the hymn '**All Creatures of our God and King**' the songwriter in stanza four, line one wrote: "For giving others take your part." Beloved parents, the secret to living is giving. God has put that asset in your hands for the benefit of mankind. A man that dies with his assets can never be remembered. John Mason in his book "the enemy called average" says: *"When you cease to contribute, you begin to die."* I pray for you that you will not die unsung in Jesus Name.

When you become relevant in your community, you give others a chance to live, and a reason to be remembered for good. God is seeking for investors in His church and not consumers. He is seeking for participants and not spectators. How relevant are you in your community? It is rewarding to be relevant.

The Centurion's servant who was dear to him was sick and was ready to die. He sent some elders to Jesus. And when they got to Jesus they begged him earnestly saying that *"the one for whom He should do this was deserving."* Why? Because the centurion had been very relevant to his community. Luke 7:5 says, *"...for he loves our nation and has built us a synagogue."* May your good works speak for you at the gates in Jesus Name Amen.

Likewise, Dorcas; The widows and less privileged in her community refused to accept the report of her death. They hurriedly called Peter to pray her back to life as they mournfully showed off the coats and garments she had made for them while she was alive. And of course, the miraculous happened. Her eyes opened, and she sat up!

May your benefactors arise to help you and your children in Jesus Name.

5. UNASHAMED INTEGRITY: Integrity is the ability, to be honest and truthful even when it is humiliating or not convenient. It is the ability to stand by your words, even when nobody is standing by you. This is where most Christians fail God. They want His blessings but live a life without integrity. Surely this is not the way to be remembered.

Today we remember Ananias and Saphira for falsehood. The psalmist says, *"Thou desiredst truth in the inward parts."* Joseph could have agreed to lie with Potiphar's wife. After all, they were alone in the room. But integrity with God and men made him flee.

Integrity makes a man justified before God (Genesis 20:5). It is one asset that needs no money, to qualify as a legacy . This is the reason why some families are considered 'good' for marriage even when they are not wealthy and other families who have money may not be considered favourably and may be avoided in the community. May your integrity bring favour and mercy to your children in Jesus Name.

Conclusion

"Life is not computed by duration but by donation." May you not leave this world without making an impact in Jesus Name. The Bible says you are the salt of the earth. You have been created to sweeten the lives of people. It is not how long you live but how well you live. What are you donating to this world? Methuselah lived 969 years on earth, and all that was remembered and recorded for him was the 969 years he lived. John the Baptist died in his youth, but today people reverence him as the forerunner of Christ. May you not live your old age regretting to leave undone what you should have done in Jesus Name.

It is what you give to your children that you will be remembered for. To make the most of life as parents, you need a healthy mind as well as a fit body. Parents should learn how to handle stress, to think more clearly and to develop your relationships with the children.

Like Pastor E.A Adeboye rightly puts it, one thing you owe your children is discipline. If you fail to give it to them, the result of the indiscipline will haunt you later in life. I pray that this will not be your portion in Jesus Name.

I am glad you have read this book. You will do well to get some copies for your friends as well. Parenting is an enterprise that comes with enviable rewards in the evening of a person's life. I counsel you to put all the principles in this book to proper use. You will share testimonies in Jesus Name. I also counsel you to attend seminars and conferences on parenting. Together let us give our children a better legacy. The Bible says our children shall be like Olive plants round about our table. Olives don't sprout overnight!

I pray that we shall all leave our footprints in the sand of times in Jesus Name. GOD BLESS YOU.

CONCLUSION

PRAYER POINTS FOR FATHERS

1. Holy Spirit, the Spirit of counsel, might and truth, partner with me as I oversee my home in the Name of Jesus Christ.

2. Oh Lord my Father, you have made me the head, let me never become the tail in my home in Jesus Name.

3. The scarcity of greatness in my life and family I reject you in Jesus name. You my destiny you will not be dragged on the floor. You my hands you are the instrument of my labour. I decree that you shall always be up and not down. You shall be sufficient for me in all good works. I will never beg for bread in Jesus Name.

4. I shall build, and I shall inhabit. I shall plant vineyards, and I shall eat the fruits of them. I shall not build for another to inhabit; I shall not plant for another to harvest. The Lord shall look in my direction WITH MERCY and make me fruitful and prosperous in the land, even in a foreign land. In Jesus Name.

5. In my old age, I will not go naked. The fire of the enemy will not burn me. My children will not be used as whips to flog me in Jesus Name.

6. In the days of my children's glories, I will not be missing. In the seasons of my children's prosperity, oh Lord decorate my life with the garment of honour in the Name of Jesus.

7. Jacob was rewarded by his son Joseph, and he took him out of famine to the land of Goshen in his old age. Oh Lord my Father, in my old age, use my children to wipe away all my years of tears and sweating and give me the reward of a husband and father in Jesus Name.

PRAYER POINTS FOR MOTHERS

1. Holy Spirit Divine, be the covering over my life and family and give us the anointing of ease to obey your divine instructions in Jesus Name.

2. You my children (Names) the hands that gave you suck, will not bury you. I have known your beginning I will not know your end in the Name of Jesus Christ.

3. Private tears, secret tears, and silent tears, over my life, my home, and my family, come to an end. The enemies will not mix sorrow to my joy. While I am still eating, it will not suddenly finish in Jesus Name Amen.

4. Where I missed it, my children will not miss it. Where I carried shame, they will carry honour. Where I carried lack, they will have abundance in Jesus name. Oh Lord, use my children to rewrite my story and reward my years of labour over them in Jesus Name.

5. Agenda of evil marital pattern in my family line, will not prosper over my children. You my children, you shall be married. You shall have a Godly marriage. You shall enjoy marriage. The fire of the enemy shall not burn you in marriage. Your seats shall not be empty and shall not be taken by another in Jesus Name.

6. In the gathering of fulfilled mothers, my head shall not be bowed in shame. My voice shall not be lost in the crowd. I shall be highly honoured. I shall be celebrated in the Name of Jesus Christ Amen

7. In the season of my rest, I shall not be wrestling with agony and pain. I shall triumph gloriously. The Lord shall give me the reward of a wife and a mother, and I shall sit back to enjoy the good fruits of my labour in Jesus Name.

www.ingramcontent.com/pod-product-compliance
Lightning Source LLC
Chambersburg PA
CBHW052052070526
44584CB00017B/2142